BEHIND
Islands in the Stream

Also by Thomas Fensch ...

Essential Elements of Steinbeck

The FBI Files on John Steinbeck

Conversations with John Steinbeck

Steinbeck and Covici:

The Story of a Friendship

The Man Who Was Dr. Seuss:

The Life and Work of Theodor Geisel

Of Sneetches and Whos and the Good Dr. Seuss: Essays on the Life and Work of Theodor Geisel

The Man Who Was Walter Mitty:

The Life and Work of James Thurber

Conversations with James Thurber

Oskar Schindler:

The Man, the Book, the Film, the Holocaust And Its Survivors

The Kennedy-Khrushchev Letters

Life, Love, Losses and Dogs:

A Memoir with Paw Prints

and others ...

BEHIND
Islands in the Stream

Hemingway, Cuba, the FBI
and the crook factory

Thomas Fensch

New Century Books

Copyright © 2009, 2019 by Thomas Fensch

All rights reserved. No part of this book many be reproduced or utilized in any form or by any means, electronic or mechanical, including photocopying or recording, or by any information storage and retrieval system, without written permission from the author and publisher.

New Century Books 8821 Rockdale Rd.
N. Chesterfield, Va, 23236-2150
newcentbks@gmail.com

ISBN 978-0-9995496-6-7 paperback
ISBN 978-0-9995496-7-4 ebook

Cover photograph, uncredited

Book design by Jill Ronsley, suneditwrite.com

Contents

Chronology:
 Key dates in the life of Ernest Hemingway 1

Introduction:
 Hemingway, Cuba, the FBI and the crook factory 7

1. The FBI Files on Ernest Hemingway 13

 A selection of the original files 129

2. Islands in the Stream 143

Denouement 157

Suggestions for Further Reading 163

About the Author 165

Chronology

Key dates in the life of Ernest Hemingway

(All Hemingway books were published by Scribners, except where noted.)

1899   Ernest Miller Hemingway is born in Oak Park, Illinois, July 21, the son of Clarence and Grace Hemingway.

1917   He graduates from high school; attempts to enlist in the Army, but is rejected because of poor vision in one eye. He gets a job as a reporter for *The Kansas City Star*; much of his abbreviated prose style, subsequently refined, is learned from newspaper journalism.

1918   Drives an ambulance during World War I, but then volunteers to supervise a Red Cross canteen. While delivering chocolates and cigarettes to the men on the front lines, he was wounded on July 8, near Fossalta di Piave, and had over 200 pieces (some say as many as 277 pieces) of shrapnel removed from his legs. He had an affair with nurse Agnes von Kurowsky, which formed the basis for his novel *A Farewell to Arms*, published in 1929.

1920   He moves to Canada and becomes a reporter for *The Toronto Star*.

1921   Hemingway marries Hadley Richardson; they move to Paris to join the community of American expatriates living there.

1922   Hemingway covers the Greco-Turkish War, as a correspondent for *The Toronto Star*. In late December Hadley loses a suitcase full of Hemingway's unpublished work in a railroad station in Paris.

1923 Hemingway's *Three Stories and Ten Poems* is published in Paris by Robert McAlmon. His first son John, is born.

1924 *in our time,* a collection of vignettes is published in Paris by Three Mountains Press.

1925 *In Our Time,* with fourteen additional stories added, is published in New York by Boni & Liveright.

1926 Hemingway had a "next work" clause in his *In Our Time* contract with Boni & Liveright. He wrote *The Torrents of Spring,* a parody of the style of Sherwood Anderson, Horace Liveright's favorite author. When Liveright rejects *The Torrents of Spring,* it is published by Maxwell Perkins at Scribners, so Scribners would have Hemingway's next novel, *The Sun Also Rises,* also published in 1926. Those books began his life-long association with Perkins and Scribners. During his lifetime, he published all his books with Scribners except *Men at War.*

1927 Hemingway divorces Hadley Richardson and marries Pauline Pfeiffer. His short story collection, *Men Without Women* is published.

1928 Hemingway and Pfeiffer move to Key West, Florida. Their son Patrick is born. Hemingway's father, Dr. Clarence Hemingway committed suicide on Dec. 6; Hemingway asks his brother to send him the gun their father used.

1929 *A Farewell to Arms* published. Hemingway had to rewrite the novel after Pauline Pfeiffer lost the first manuscript.

1931 Hemingway's third son Gregory is born. All three sons figure prominently in his novel *Islands in the Stream* published in 1970.

1932 *Death in the Afternoon,* his nonfiction study of bullfighting, is published.

1933 His short story collection, *Winner Take Nothing,* is published.

1935 *Green Hills of Africa* is published.

1936 A short story, "On the Blue Water," is published, which includes an incident that Hemingway will later expand into *The Old Man and the Sea*. Two of his most famous short stories, "The Snows of Kilimanjaro" and "The Short Happy Life of Francis Macomber" are published.

1937 He becomes a war correspondent covering the Spanish Civil War and works to collect funds for the Republican side. *To Have and Have Not* is published.

1938 He collaborates with Joris Ivens on the film *The Spanish Earth,* about the Loyalist side of the Spanish Civil War. *The Fifth Column and the First Forty-nine Stories* and *The Short Stories of Ernest Hemingway* are published.

1939 He rents Finca Vigia ("Lookout Farm", sometimes translated as "Watchtower farm") outside Havana, for a year.

1940 Hemingway divorces Pauline Pfeiffer and marries Martha Gellhorn, herself a writer. They purchase Finca Vigia which becomes their home. Hemingway will live in Cuba for the next 20-plus years and produce much of his best work there. *For Whom the Bell Tolls* is published.

1942 Hemingway establishes *the crook factory,* his organization of anti-Nazi operators. Guns are installed on the Pilar and he begins hunting Nazi submarines. *Men at War: The Best War Stories of All Time* is published by Crown publishers.

1942 –1943 He lives in Cuba and patrols the Caribbean waters on his motor yacht, Pilar, looking for Nazi submarines; this forms the basis for the last segment of his novel *Islands in the Stream* published in 1970.

1944 He meets correspondent Mary Welsh in London and travels with American troops in France and Germany as a World War Two correspondent and famously "liberates" the bar of the Hotel Ritz in Paris.

1945 Hemingway and Martha Gellhorn are divorced. Reputedly she left him to maintain her own writing career and not to remain "Mrs. Ernest Hemingway."

1946 Hemingway marries Mary Welsh, his fourth wife.

1947 Hemingway receives the Bronze Star for his role in the liberation of Paris, awarded at the American Embassy, Havana, June 16.

1950 *Across the River and into the Trees* is published, one of his critically least successful books.

1952 *The Old Man and the Sea* is published, his shortest and widely considered one of his best novels.

1953 Hemingway wins the Pulitzer Prize for fiction, specifically for *The Old Man and the Sea*. He goes hunting in east Africa and survives *two* near-fatal airplane crashes. His airplane crashes in Uganda; he and his party are transferred to a rescue airplane, which then also crashes. His obituary is flashed around the world.

1954 Hemingway wins the Nobel Prize for Literature for the body of his work.

1960 The Hemingways move to Ketchum, Idaho. He is hospitalized at the Mayo Clinic suffering from uncontrolled high blood pressure, liver disease, diabetes and depression. He receives electro-shock treatments, which largely destroy his ability to write.

1961 Hemingway commits suicide early July 2, by using one of his shotguns, for a single shot to the head. He was buried in Ketchum, Idaho.

POSTHUMOUS PUBLICATIONS

1964 *A Moveable Feast,* his memoirs of his years in Paris is published, using his spelling *moveable* for *movable*.

1967 *By-Line Ernest Hemingway,* edited by William White, is published.

1969 *The Fifth Column and Four Stories of the Spanish Civil War* is published.

1970 *Islands in the Stream* is published, his novel which culminates in searching for Nazi submarines in the Caribbean waters off Cuba.

1972 *The Nick Adams Stories* is published.

1979 *88 Poems,* edited by Nicolas Gerogiannis, is published by Harcourt Brace.

1981 *Ernest Hemingway: Selected Letters* is published, edited by Carlos Baker.

1983 *The Complete Poems* (revised edition) is published by the University of Nebraska Press.

1985 *The Dangerous Summer,* a nonfiction book about bullfighters, is published.

1986 *The Garden of Eden* is published.

1987 *The Complete Stories of Ernest Hemingway: The Finca Vigia Edition* is published as the definitive version of his best stories.

1999 *True at First Light,* about hunting in Africa, is published.

2005 *Under Kilimanjaro* is published by Kent State University Press; a longer variant of *True at First Light.* Many believe it is the last publishable Hemingway manuscript extant.

2009 *A Moveable Feast* is revised and re-edited by Hemingway's grandson, Sean Hemingway and re-published by Scribners. All Scribners Hemingway titles are repackaged in new covers.

Introduction

Hemingway, Cuba, the FBI and the crook factory

Ernest Hemingway lived in Cuba, at Finca Vigia — "Lookout Farm" — for 20-plus years, 1939–1940- to 1960. Half his productive life as a writer was spent there. And while there, he wrote some of his very best novels. And one of his worst.

They included part of *For Whom the Bell Tolls, Across the River and into the Trees, A Moveable Feast, The Old Man and the Sea* and *Islands in the Stream.*

There are several books worth studying for Hemingway's life during these two decades, but the one most crucial is *Hemingway in Cuba,* by Norberto Fuentes. First published in Cuba in 1982 under the title *Hemingway — Our Own,* it was translated into English and published in the United States in 1984. It is a rich trove of material about Hemingway, Cuba, and his friends and compatriots. No comprehensive understanding of Hemingway's life there is possible without *Hemingway in Cuba.*

Fuentes writes that in Cuba, during the period of the end of the Spanish Civil War, there were about 3,000 Spanish Falangists (Spanish fascists) in Cuba, most pro-Nazi.

But U.S. Ambassador to Cuba Spruille Braden later wrote in his memoirs, *Diplomats and Demagogues,* that there were

300,000 Spaniards in wartime Cuba, of whom 15,000 to 30,000 were "violent Falangists." (Braden, in *Hemingway: A Biography*, by Jeffrey Meyers, pp. 368.)

Hemingway rounded up a ragtag organization to spy on the Cuban Falangists and report, through him, to the American Ambassador Braden, said to be the best U.S. Cuban Ambassador ever posted to Havana. Hemingway named this amateur spy operation *the crook factory*.

They were, according to Jeffrey Meyers, "priests, waiters, fishermen, whores, pimps and bums." (Meyers, pp. 368.)

Alternatively, in his biography of Hemingway, only a few pages later, Meyers writes: "According to the Cuban newspapers, the outfit was made up of monarchists, aristocrats, priests, bartenders, criminals and whores." (pp. 384)

Ambassador Spruille Braden said that Hemingway "enlisted a bizarre combination of Spaniards: some bar tenders; a few wharf rats; some down-at-the-heel pelota players and former bullfighters; two Basque priests, assorted exiled counts and dukes, several Loyalists and Francistas. He built up an excellent organization and did an A-One job." (Braden *Diplomats and Demagogues*, pp. 282–4, quoted in Reynolds, pp. 60.)

That operation was eventually curtailed by Braden, but it led to Hemingway's patrols searching for Nazi submarines, on his motor yacht, the Pilar, in the waters off Cuba.

Terry Mort writes that *Pilar* was Hemingway's nickname for his second wife, Pauline Pfeiffer Hemingway. Or it could have been the name of a shrine that Hemingway knew about, in Zaragoza, where he watched bullfights. (Mort, pp. 51) The yacht named after the shrine would have been easier to explain to wives number three and four …, Mort suggests.

And those patrols furnished him the material for the end third of what would become the novel *Islands in the Stream*.

His patrols in the Pilar not only had the blessing of Ambassador Braden, but were financed, gasoline and armaments, by the U.S. Embassy. And here the narrative gets darker, for the FBI deeply resented these covert Embassy-Hemingway operations. Hoover's FBI believed Hemingway was treading on its turf and was a security threat. *And* was also a Communist fellow traveler, a member of so-called "Communist front organizations."

And while Hemingway and his crook factory tracked the Falangists and later searched for Nazi submarines in the Caribbean, the FBI tracked Hemingway.

Fuentes tells much of this story with grace and verve; Hemingway was, during those two decades, the most beloved public figure in Havana and in all of Cuba. He was especially venerated because he was living in Cuba when he won the Nobel Prize for Literature.

Hemingway thought the number nine lucky, so the Pilar had nine crew members. Fuentes writes:

> It is easy to understand how Hemingway was able to enlist nine men in his adventure, a since it seemed to be such an attractive project, offering some possibility for real action and much for having a good time. As the captain, Hemingway was zealous in his duties, however, and he made his selection among men he considered to be in tune with the operation. That is why he picked a sprinkling of strong jai-alai players, that violent sport of which he had been a fan since his first trip to Spain. They would guarantee the muscle necessary to throw their grenades down the hatchway of the submarines when they surfaced. (pp. 194)

He also writes:

> Although he did not score any victory, Hemingway was able to put together a fairly efficient military unit with official backing, an operative combat organization of which he was the captain and in which he had enlisted men who shared his own life style. Moreover, he was participating in an adventure in which terms like "confidential," "paramilitary" and "intelligence missions" were used, whose official nature served to mask adolescent yearnings for heroic actions for which Hemingway succeeded in enlisting not only the folkloric characters who were his companions on his pleasure rounds in Havana, but two intelligence officers and one American ambassador as well. (pp. 193)

Of particular value in *Hemingway in Cuba* is a one page-plus chart, set in a two-column format; on the left column is the real name of a crewman on the Pilar, on the right is the character name in *Islands in the Stream* (pp. 207–209).

Funetes mentions the FBI only once: there is a one sentence statement that Hemingway biographer Jeffrey Meyers found the secret FBI files on Hemingway.

When Hemingway established his crook factory, many around him assumed it was merely amusing child's play. But the FBI files tell a different story and may well have astonished biographer Jeffrey Meyers. In *Hemingway: A Biography*, published in 1985, he writes:

> The 124-page FBI file on Hemingway cast quite a different and more menacing light on this episode. It showed that the Bureau resented his amateur but alarming intrusion into their territory; that it unsuccessfully attempted to control, mock and vilify him; that it feared his personal prestige and political power. The file was

extremely repetitive, and became unintentionally funny when the solemn bureaucrats reported the bizarre behavior of the author. Their stilted letters seem written on a typewriter by a typewriter. Thought there were ludicrous elements in this story, the file revealed that Hemingway, the American Embassy in Havana, the State Department in Washington and the FBI took the crook factory quite seriously. (pp. 367)

Hoover's FBI was not able to completely conquer Hemingway during the crook factory days (and the sub-chasing days), as Hemingway was at the height of his power and fame in Cuba and had the papal blessing of Ambassador Spruille Braden. But, as Meyers writes:

> Though Hemingway won the first round with the FBI and shifted to sub hunting after the Crook Factory was (as planned) dismantled after eight months, the FBI kept watch on him for the rest of his life. They maintained surveillance, collected information and waited for the moment to strike. (pp. 384)

The FBI kept watch on him for the rest of his life.

This book then, is the dark back story of Hemingway, Cuba, the FBI and the crook factory and Hemingway's roman a clef, *Islands in the Stream*.

We have made every effort to reprint these files accurately, but in some cases, words, numbers and other textual material is garbled. Magnifying the problem area only makes the garble larger, but does not clarify it. In some cases, matching the text before and after the garble would offer a logical solution to fill in a sentence, but some numbers and foreign words are problematical.

The Bibliography offers additional material on Hemingway, his world and those times.

—Thomas Fensch
Ashland, Va.
July, 2009

1
The FBI Files on Ernest Hemingway

The first letter in the FBI files is dated October 8, 1942 and was sent to the FBI from the Legal Attache at the American Embassy, Havana. The Legal Attache was, in fact, an FBI agent.

Havana, Cuba
October 8, 1942

Director,
Federal Bureau of Investigation
Washington, D.C.

Re: ERNEST HEMINGWAY

Dear Sir;

The writer desires to acquaint the Bureau, in detail, with a relationship that has developed under the direction of the Ambassador with MR. ERNEST HEMINGWAY.

As the Bureau is aware, HEMINGWAY has been resident in Cuba almost continuously during the past two years, occupying his private finca at San Francisco de Paula, about 14 miles east of Havana.

Mr. HEMINGWAY has been on friendly terms with Consul KENNETH POTTER since the spring of 1941; recently he has become very friendly with Mr. ROBERT P. JOYCE, Second Secretary of Embassy, and through Mr. JOYCE, has met the Ambassador on several occasions. It is the writer's observation that the initiative in developing these friendships has come from HEMINGWAY, but the opportunity of association with him has been welcomed by Embassy officials.

At several conferences with the Ambassador and officers of the Embassy late in August, 1942, the topic of utilizing HEMINGWAY'S services in intelligence activities was discussed. The Ambassador pointed out that HEMINGWAY'S experiences during the Spanish Civil War, his intimate acquaintances with Spanish Republican refugees in Cuba, as well as his long experience on this island, seemed to place him in a position of great usefulness to the Embassy's intelligence program. While this program is inclusive of all intelligence agencies and the Embassy's own sources of information, the fact is that the Ambassador regards to Bureau representation in the Embassy as the unit primarily concerned in this work. The Ambassador further pointed out that HEMINGWAY had completed some writing which had occupied him until that time, and was now ready and anxious to be called upon.

The writer pointed out at these conferences that any information which could be secured concerning the operation of the Spanish Falange in Cuba would be of material assistance in our work, and that if HEMINGWAY was willing to devote his time and abilities to the gathering of such information, the result would be most welcome to us. It was pointed out to Mr. JOYCE, who is designated by the Ambassador as the Embassy's coordinator of intelligence activities, that some consideration should be given to the question of relationship between Mr. HEMINGWAY and the Bureau representatives directly.

This question existed in the writer's mind for two reasons: (1) It is recalled that when the Bureau was attacked early in 1940 as a result of the arrests in Detroit of certain individuals charged with Neutrality Act violations for fostering enlistments in the Spanish Republican forces, Mr. HEMINGWAY was among the signers of a declaration which severely criticized the Bureau in that case; (2) in attendance at a Jai Alai match with HEMINGWAY, the writer was introduced by him to a friend as a member of the Gestapo, On that occasion, I told HEMINGWAY that I did not appreciate the Introduction, whereupon he promptly corrected himself and said I was one of the United States Consuls.

Mr. JOYCE made inquiries of HEMINGWAY concerning his attitude toward working with us, without disclosing the reasons therefor, and reported his attitude appeared to be entirely favorable to the Bureau; that he was unable to remember any details of the Detroit incident of 1940, and that he regarded the Gestapo introduction as a jest.

It was decided, nevertheless, that HEMINGWAY would work directly in contact with Mr. JOYCE and not with this writer; this suggestion came from Mr. JOYCE, and no advantage was seen in making any different arrangements. It was also decided that the expenses he would incur would be paid by the Embassy directly out of specials funds.

Consequently, early in September, 1942, ERNEST HEMINGWAY began to engage directly in intelligence activities on behalf of the American Embassy in Havana. These activities he manages from his finca, with visits to Havana two or three times weekly. He is operating through Spanish Republicans whose identities have not been furnished but which we are assured are obtainable when desired. At a meeting with him at his finca on September 30, 1942, the writer was advised that he now has four men operating on a full time basis, and 14 more whose positions are barmen, waiters, and the like, operating on a part-time basis. The cost of this program is approximately $500 a month. Reports are submitted to HEMINGWAY, who dictates the material to a personal secretary and furnishes duplicate copies to Mr. JOYCE, one being for the embassy and the other for our use. The material so far submitted appears to be carefully prepared and set out, and the Ambassador has noted on several memoranda that he likes HEMINGWAY'S approach, and wishes to encourage him in the type of work he is doing. HEMINGWAY himself told me that he declined an offer from Hollywood to write a script for a "March of Time" report on the "Flying Tigers" in Burma, for which the compensation was to be $150,000, because he considers the work he is now engaged in as of greater importance.

One of the aspects of Mr. HEMINGWAY'S relationship with the Embassy (approximately one and one-third lines redacted here) to utilize his services for certain coastal patrol and investigative work on the east coast of Cuba. HEMINGWAY, who has a wide reputation as a fisherman, knows the coast line and waters of Cuba very intimately; he has also engaged over a 12-year period in some scientific investigations concerning the migration of Marlin on behalf of the Museum of Natural History, New York City (One and a third-lines redacted here) has acceded to HEMINGWAY's request for authorization to patrol certain areas where submarine activity has been reported, (about three-fourth of one line redacted here) and an allotment of gasoline is now being obtained for his use. He has requested (one line and a fourth of a second line redacted) he has secured from the Ambassador a promise that his crew members will be recognized as war casualties for the purposes of indemnification in the event of any loss of life results from this operation.

With specific reference to the conducting of intelligence investigations on the island of Cuba by Mr. HEMINGWAY, the writer wishes to state that his interest thus far has not been limited to the Spanish Falange and Spanish activities, but that he has included numerous German suspects. His reports are promptly furnished and he assures Mr. JOYCE that is only desire is to be of assistance on a cooperative basis, without compensation to himself, and that he will be guided at all times by our wishes. So far, no conflict has developed between his work and that which Bureau personnel is handling in Havana, and HEMINGWAY told me that he wishes to be told where to limit his investigations whenever this is thought desirable.

The Bureau will be continuously advised of pertinent developments in this situation, Meanwhile, if there is any information or instructions for the guidance of the writer, I would appreciate being advised.

Very truly yours,
R. G. LEDDY
Legal Attache

Leddy files a second letter to the FBI the next day, regarding Hemingway.

Havana, Cuba
October 9, 1942

PERSONAL AND CONFIDENTIAL

Director,
Federal Bureau of Investigation
Washington, D.C.

Re: ERNEST HEMINGWAY

Dear Sir;

Reference is made to my letter dated October 8, 1942 in this matter. For the further information of the Bureau regarding Mr. HEMINGWAY'S participation in intelligence activities, under the auspices of the Embassy, it is now understood that one GUSTAVO DURAN is being sent from Washington for the special purpose of assisting Mr. HEMINGWAY in this work.

Mr. HEMINGWAY advised the Ambassador that DURAN had been active with him in intelligence work on the Republican side of the Spanish Civil War, and recommended his abilities very highly. DURAN, he said, held some position in the Department of State, the exact position being unknown. He was uncertain whether DURAN was formerly a Spanish citizen had acquired American citizenship.

At the instance of Mr. HEMINGWAY, the Ambassador communicated with the Department of State which agreed to release DURAN on leave of absence in order that he might come to Cuba and work with Mr. HEMINGWAY as he did in Spain.

Of further interest in this matter is a visit of Mrs. ERNEST HEMINGWAY (the former MARTHA GELLHORN) to Washington during the week commencing October 12, 1942. Mrs. HEMINGWAY is to be the personal guest of Mrs. ROOSEVELT during her stay in Washington, and the

Ambassador outlined to her certain aspects of the intelligence situation in Cuba in order that she might convey the same, in personal conversation, to the President and Mrs. ROOSEVELT. This has specific reference to the Embassy's request for approval of financing by the American Government of (illegible) and investigative program brought out by the Cuban authorities. To date, no action has resulted from Washington on this proposal and it is thought by the Ambassador that some results may be obtained through this form of personal contact.

In view of the importance of this matter, you may desire to bring this and reference letter to the personal attention of the Director.

Very truly yours,
R.G. LEDDY
Legal Attache

The FBI apparently had a number of agents/informants specified as S.I.S. This abbreviation may be Secret Intelligence Service, originally a British spy term. The exact number of these agents is unknown. They are usually only identified as S.I.S. and an agent number.

Washington FBI administrator D.M. Ladd received a memo from S.I.S. agent #396 on Dec. 8, 1942. That informant may well be Leddy, the Legal Attache in the Embassy staff in Havana. D. M. Ladd, in the FBI administration in Washington, prepared the following memo for J. Edgar Hoover Dec. 11, 1942.

THE DIRECTOR

RE: ERNEST HEMINGWAY

<u>BACKGROUND</u> CONF. INFT. S.I.S. #<u>396</u>

(Almost one line black)
Havana, Cuba, has advised that Ernest Hemingway, a well known writer, has been employed by the American Embassy as a confidential informant.

<u>FACTS</u>

Hemingway is on friendly terms with certain member of the Embassy staff, specifically with the United States Consul Kenneth Potter and with Mr. Robert P. Hoyce, Second Secretary of the Embassy. Ambassador Braden is also on very friendly terms with Hemingway and apparently is "sold" on him and (illegible) complete confidence in him.

It was thought that when Hemingway became an informant of the Embassy that he probably would supply much information of value concerning the operation of the Spanish Falange. Mr. Hemingway has worked directly in contact with Mr. Joyce and now with CONF. INFT. S.I.S. #<u>396</u>

It was thought that when the Bureau was attacked early in 1940 as a result of the arrests in Detroit of certain individuals charged with neutrality act violations for fostering enlistments in the Spanish Republican forces, Mr. Hemingway was among the signers of a declaration which severely criticized the Bureau in that case. Hemingway has since stated that he has forgotten that incident.

Since Hemingway has become an Embassy informant, he has organized a group of operators whose identities are not known and who engage in investigative work. The reports of these operators' investigations are furnished to the office of the Legal Attache. Hemingway and his staff have embarked on investigations of all types and not merely on the Spanish Falange. One such investigation has General Benites as the subject.

(About a fourth of a line blank) further (illegible) that Hemingway has access to official Embassy records (blank) stated that although he has insisted that copies of Bureau reports should not be shown to anyone except a limited number of Embassy officials, it is quite apparent that at least the contents, if not the reports themselves are known to Mr. Hemingway.

An individual by the name of Gustavo Duran, who aids Hemingway in his investigations, is employed and paid by the State department. Duran's operations and attitude, in direct relation to Mr. Joyce, assume proportions of domination and direction rather than assistance to the agencies properly engaged in investigating subversive activities. The organization operated by Hemingway is reported to be unknown for its reliability or trustworthiness. According to our information, data is transmitted to him without an official check being made on what happens to this information thereafter.

(about four words blanked out) advised that he has not as yet opposed Mr. Hemingway's services but had thought best to let the situation work itself out as long as no direct conflict with the Bureau's work occurred, in view of the friendly feeling and mutual understanding between the Embassy and Hemingway.

ACTION

(One complete paragraph redacted, about five or six lines.)

Respectfully,

D.M. Ladd

Ladd prepares another report on the Hemingway-Cuba situation for J. Edgar Hoover. The material underlined appears to have been underlined in pencil.

Federal Bureau of Investigation
United States Department of Justice
Washington, D.C.
December 17, 1942

MEMORANDUM FOR THE DIRECTOR

RE: ERNEST HEMINGWAY

BACKGROUND:

Mr. Ernest Hemingway, well-known American writer, recently has been acting as personal informant of Ambassador Spruille Braden, in Havana, Cuba.

DETAILS:

FBI Attache R.G. Leddy, stationed at the American Embassy in Havana, Cuba, has recently advised that Ernest Hemingway, well-known American writer, has been residing in Cuba, just outside Havana, for approximately two years. Hemingway, it will be recalled, engaged actively on the side of the Spanish Republic during the Spanish Civil War, and it is reported that he is very well acquainted with a large number of Spanish refugees in Cuba and elsewhere. Hemingway, it will be recalled, joined in attacking the Bureau early in 1940, at the time of the "general smear campaign" following the arrests of certain individuals in Detroit charged with violation of Federal statues in connection with their participation in Spanish Civil War activities. It will be recalled that Hemingway signed a declaration, along with a number of other individuals, severely criticizing the Bureau in connection with the Detroit arrests. Hemingway has been accused of being of Communist sympathy, although we are advised that he has denied and does vigorously deny any Communist affiliation or sympathy. Hemingway is reported to be personally friendly with Ambassador Braden, and he is reported to enjoy the Ambassador's complete confidence. According to Agent Leddy, Hemingway is also on very friendly terms with United States Consul Kenneth Potter, presently stationed in Cuba, and with Mr. Robert P. Joyce, Second Secretary of the American Embassy in Havana.

Mr. Leddy has advised that Hemingway has been acting as an informant of Ambassador Braden for the past several months and in this capacity has been dealing closely with Ambassador Braden and Second Secretary Joyce. Leddy stated that Ambassador Braden has made no secret of this connection, in so far as Agent Leddy is concerned, and, further, that the Ambassador has instructed that all of Hemingway's reports and any information furnished by him must be turned over to Mr. Leddy.

Mr. Leddy has advised that the original arrangement whereby Mr. Hemingway would act as an informant of Ambassador Braden was largely concerned with certain political matters, particularly as to the connection or alleged connection of certain Cuban political leaders with the Spanish Falange and the involvement of Cuban officials generally in local graft and corruption within Cuba. Ambassador Braden, as you will recall, is a very impulsive individual and he apparently has a "bee in his bonnet" for some time concerning alleged graft and has stated that Mr. Hemingway has apparently organized a number of informants among the Spanish refugee group, whose intentions are not known to Leddy, and, according to the best of his information, their identities are not known to anyone except Hemingway.

Agent Leddy has advised that Hemingway's activities have branched out and that he and his informants are now engaged in reporting to the Embassy various types of information concerning subversive activities generally. Mr. Leddy stated that he has become quite concerned with respect to Hemingway's activities and that they are undoubtedly going to be very embarrassing unless something is done to put a stop to them, <u>Mr. Leddy has advised that Hemingway is apparently undertaking a rather involved investigation with regard to Cuban officials prominently connected with the Cuban government, including General Manuel (illegible), head of the Cuban National Police, that he. Agent Leddy, is sure that the Cubans are eventually going to find out about this if Hemingway continues operating, and that serious trouble may result.</u>

Mr. Leddy has advised that there is an individual attached to the Embassy by the name of Gustavo Duran, who is of Spanish descent and is employed by the Coordinator of Inter-American Affairs; that Duran is a very close friend of Hemingway and is apparently consulting and actually working with Hemingway in connection with the latter's activities.

This matter has been discussed at some length with Mr. Leddy, and he was asked just what objection, if any, he has ever personally or officially offered to the arrangement or whether he has discussed its possible bad effects with the Ambassador.

<u>Leddy stated that he has not offered any objection whatsoever to this proposition:</u> that the Ambassador has advised Leddy quite frankly and openly that Hemingway is the Ambassador's informant and that all information of any kind whatsoever furnished by Hemingway will be immediately turned over to Leddy, which, according to Leddy, is actually being done. Leddy suggested that the Bureau take this matter up with Ambassador Braden while he is in the United States.

It was pointed out to Leddy that the Bureau certainly cannot take the matter up with Ambassador Braden and protest to him unless Leddy has first made the Bureau's position quite plain to the Ambassador himself. It was pointed out to Mr. Leddy that the Ambassador would undoubtedly resent any complaint and protest could only be based upon Leddy's recommendations and information, unless Leddy has himself first discussed the matter with the Ambassador and pointed out the Bureau's position, this being particularly true inasmuch as Ambassador Braden has apparently been quite frank with Agent Leddy about the arrangement and has insisted that all information furnished by Hemingway be immediately furnished to Agent Leddy.

(One complete paragraph redacted here; approximately 12 lines.)

Mr. Leddy stated that he can point out to the Ambassador that he, Leddy, has not checked any reports from Hemingway concerning corruption in the Cuban Government; that he does not feel that Bureau agents should become involved in any such investigations, it being entirely without our jurisdiction and a matter in which the Cubans themselves alone are concerned and something that, if we get involved in it, is going to mean that all of us will be thrown out of Cuba, "bag and baggage."

Agent Leddy stated he can point out to the Ambassador the extreme danger of having some informant like Hemingway given free rein got stir up trouble such as that which will undoubtedly ensue if this situation continues. Mr. Leddy stated that despite the fact the Ambassador likes Hemingway and apparently has confidence in him, he is of the option that he, Leddy, can handle this situation with the Ambassador so that Hemingway's services as an informant will be completely discontinued. Mr. Leddy stated that he can point out to the Ambassador that Hemingway is going further than just an informant; that he actually branching out into an investigative organization of his own which is not subject to any control whatsoever.

RECOMMENDATION

(One complete paragraph redacted here; approximately six to eight lines.)

Mr. Leddy, if you approve, will be told to advise the Bureau promptly and in detail as to the outcome of his negotiations with the Ambassador concerning this matter, at which time we should, it is believed, advise Mr. Berle for the Bureau's protection.

Respectfully,

D.M. Ladd

On December 17, 1942, J. Edgar Hoover sends a reply to a recipient in Havana. The earlier Dec. 5, 1942 letter from Havana apparently no longer exists.

December 17, 1942

PERSONAL AND CONFIDENTIAL
VIA DIPLOMATIC AIR POUCH

CONF. INFT. S.I.S. #396

RE: ERNEST HEMINGWAY

Dear Sir;

Reference is made to your memorandum dated December 5, 1942, regarding Ernest Hemingway's employment by the American Embassy as a confidential informant and his activities in relation thereto.

In view of the trust and friendship (illegible) in Hemingway by Embassy officials, you are instructed to discuss diplomatically with Ambassador Braden the disadvantages which you pointed out in your above referred to memorandum in relation to Hemingway's activities in Cuba. It should be stressed that because of the confidential nature contained in the Bureau's reports and the necessity of safeguarding its informants that it is unwise to allow anyone who is not a Government official to have access to the information contained in your files. In this connection it is pointed out that information is transmitted to you directly from the Bureau which was gained from confidential sources in the United States and elsewhere, and it is absolutely necessary that these sources of information be protected.

Any information which you may have relating to the unreliability of Ernest Hemingway as an informant may be discreetly brought to the attention of Ambassador Braden. In this respect it will be recalled that recently Hemingway gave information concerning the refueling of submarines in Caribbean waters which proved unreliable.

I desire that you furnish me at an early date the results of your conversations with Ambassador Braden concerning Ernest Hemingway and his aides and their activities.

Very truly yours,
John Edgar Hoover
Director

On December 19, 1942, J. Edgar Hoover sends a memo to two subordinates; the entire memo is typed in Italic type and appears to be typed on blank paper; there is no FBI letterhead of any sort on the memo.

The end of the first paragraph appears to he pure unvarnished Hoover.

The reference in the third paragraph to "some message had been sent to him, The President, by Hemingway, through a mutual friend..." may well have been by Martha Gellhorn, during her visit with the Roosevelts.

The left side of the last line in the final paragraph (in the original) is illegible: it appears to be "but impress Mr. Berle with the fact that ------- ant to become involved..."

"... with the fact that we do not want to become involved..." appears to be a reasonable reading of the illegible material.

December 19, 1942

MEMORANDUM FOR MR. TAMM
MR. LADD

In regard to Mr. Ladd's memorandum of the 17th instant concerning the use of Ernest Hemingway by the United States Ambassador to Cuba, I of course realize the complete undesireability of this sort of a connection or relationship. Certainly Hemingway is the last man, in my estimation, to be used in any such capacity. His judgment is not of the best, and if his sobriety is the same as it was some years ago, that is certainly questionable.

However, I do not think there is anything we should do in this matter, nor do I think our representative in Havana should do anything about it with the Ambassador. The Ambassador is somewhat hot-headed and I haven't the slightest doubt that he would immediately tell Hemingway of the objections raised by the FBI. Hemingway has no particular love for the FBI and would no doubt embark upon a campaign of vilification.

In addition thereto, you will recall that in my conference recently with the President, he indicated that some message had been sent to him, The President, by Hemingway, through a mutual friend and Hemingway was insisting that one-half million dollars be granted to the Cuban authorities so that they could take care of internees.

I do not see that it is a matter that directly affects out relationship as long as Hemingway does not report directly to us or we deal directly with him. Anything which he gives to the Ambassador which the Ambassador in turns forwards to us, we can accept without any impropriety.

I have no objections to Mr. Tamm informally talking with Mr. Berle about this matter, but impress Mr. Berle with the fact that we do not want to become involved in any controversial concerns.

Very truly yours

John Edgar Hoover

Director

The files jump into mid-spring, 1943. The name is redacted at the bottom of this memorandum, but the same S.I.S. agent number appears at the bottom of the memorandum.

Office of the Legal Attache

Embassy of the
United States of America
Havana, Cuba

April 21, 1943

Director,
Federal Bureau of Investigation,
Washington D.C.

RE: ERNEST HEMINGWAY

Dear Sir;

The Bureau has previously been advised of the activities of Mr. Ernest Hemingway in the operation of an under cover "intelligence" organization in Cuba, under the auspices of the American Embassy.

The writer has been advised in confidence by an Embassy official that Hemingway's organization was disbanded and its work terminated as of April 1, 1943. This action was taken by the American Ambassador without any consultation or notice to representatives of the Federal Bureau of Investigation.

A complete report on the activities of Mr. Hemingway and the organization which he operated is now being prepared, and will be forwarded to the Bureau in the immediate future.

Very truly yours,
(name redacted)

CONF. INFT. S.I.S. #396

On April 27, 1943 D.M. Ladd sends the following memorandum to J. Edgar Hoover. In the last paragraph, he writes: "The Bureau has conducted no investigation of Hemingway..." but then attaches a 14-page single-spaced summary of Hemingway's activities.

This is the first time the FBI has accused Hemingway of being a Communist. Material underlined appeared to be underlined in pencil.

"The Bureau has conducted no investigation of..." are the exact words said about John Steinbeck, but the FBI files on Steinbeck began in 1942 and only ended in mid-1965 (See The FBI Files on John Steinbeck, passim).

The first few words at the beginning of the second-to-the last paragraph have been redacted, and CONF INFT S.I.S. #396 appears to have been stamped onto the page with a rubber stamp.

Material underlined appears to have been underlined in pencil.

Federal Bureau of Investigation
United States Department of Justice
Washington, D.C.

April 27, 1943

MEMORANDUM FOR THE DIRECTOR

RE: ERNEST HEMINGWAY

In accordance with your request, here is attached a memorandum which summaries the information in our files regarding Ernest Hemingway, the author.

Mr. Hemingway, it will be noted, has been connected with various so-called Communist front organizations and was active in aiding the Loyalist cause in Spain. In the latter connection he spent sometime in Spain during the Spanish revolution and reported the events transpiring there for the North American Newspaper Alliance.

Despite Hemingway's activities, no information has been received which would definitely tie him with the Communist Party or which would indicate that he is or has been a Party member. His actions, however, have indicated that his views are "liberal" and that he may be inclined favorably to Communist political philosophies.

Hemingway is now in Havana, Cuba where he has resided for over two years. For sometime he has acted as an under-cover informant for American Ambassador Spruille Braden and apparently enjoyed the Ambassador's complete confidence. You will recall that on December 17, 1942, there was set forth in a memorandum for you, the details of Hemingway's activities in Cuba, as well as the details of his association with the American Ambassador.

Briefly, Hemingway has established what was termed "an amateur information service," and gathered alleged intelligence data which he turned over to Mr. Braden. In this work, Hemingway developed his own confidential informants and was said to be friendly with a number of Spanish refugees in Cuba. His relationship with the Ambassador was quite friendly, but the Ambassador was perfectly frank with the Bureau representatives in Havana regarding this relationship and made all of the information which Hemingway furnished to him, available to the Bureau. These date, however, were almost without fail valueless.

CONF. INFT. S.I.S. #<u>396</u> the Bureau representative stationed with the American Embassy in Havana, Cuba has recently advised that the Ambassador discontinued Hemingway's services effective April 1, 1943. At the present time he is alleged to be performing <u>a highly secret naval operation for the Navy Department</u>. In this connection, the Navy Department is said to be paying the expenses for the operation of Hemingway's boat, furnishing him with arms and charting courses in the Cuban area.

The Bureau has conducted no investigation of Hemingway, but his name has been mentioned in connection with other Bureau investigations and various data concerning him have been submitted voluntarily by a number of different sources.

Respectfully,

D.M. Ladd

A 14-page FBI profile devoted to Hemingway bears the same date: April 27, 1943. It is divided into five major sections: A. Personal History and Background; Activities on Behalf of Loyalist Spain (with 11 separate sections); C. Possible Connections with Communist Party; D. Miscellaneous Activities (with four sections) and E. General Information. The entire pamphlet appears here; we have not made an attempt to reproduce the same pagination.

The FBI has Hemingway's marriage chronology wrong; there is no reference to Hadley Richardson, his first wife, unless there is a reference in material now redacted. Even if Hadley Richardson is mentioned in redacted material, the following still appears in error: FBI documents not redacted imply that Pauline Pfeiffer was his first wife — "Hemingway allegedly had a passionate love affair with Martha Gellhorn, which subsequently led to his divorce from his first wife," Section A, paragraph four.

Pauline Pfeiffer and Martha Gellhorn are mentioned in order, but they were his second and third wives.

ERNEST HEMINGWAY

TABLE OF CONTENTS

	PAGE
A. Personal History and Background	1, 2
B. Activities on Behalf of Loyalist Spain	3, 4, 5
Abraham Lincoln Brigade	5, 6, 7
American Rescue Ship Mission	7
Emergency Conference to Save Spanish Refugees	8
Joint Anti-Fascist Refugee Committee	8
Medical Bureau to Aid Spanish Democracy	8
Motion Picture Artists Committee	8
North American Committee to Aid Spanish Democracy	9
Spanish Refugee Relief Campaign	9
United Spanish Aid Committee	9
United Youth Committee to Aid Spanish Democracy	9
Writers and Artists Ambulance Corps	10
C. Possible Connections with Communist Party	10, 11
D. Miscellaneous Activities	
American Committee for the Protection of Foreign Born	12
American Writers Congress	12
League of American Writers	13
Mexican Trip	14
E. General Information	14

ERNEST HEMINGWAY

PERSONAL HISTORY AND BACKGROUND

Mr. Hemingway was born in Oak Park, Illinois on July 21, 1898, the son of Clarence Edmonds and Grace (Hall) Hemingway. He was educated in public schools and according to The New York Times of January 12, was an ambulance driver with the Italian army during the World War. He has devoted his subsequent endeavors to writing and has acquired an international reputation as an author, his best recent work being "For Whom the Bell Tolls." Other works include "Three Stories and Ten Poems" 1923, "In Our Times" 1924, "The Torrents of Spring" 1926, "The Sun Also Rises" 1926, "Men Without Women" 1927, "A Farewell to Arms" 1929, "Death in the Afternoon" 1932, "Winner Take Nothing" 1933, "Green Hills of Africa" 1935, "To Have and Have Not" 1937, "The Fifth Column and the First 49" 1938.

He has also contributed to Scribner's, Atlantic Monthly, New Republic, Esquire, Cosmopolitan and other magazines. In addition, he has had articles published in The New Masses, his "Fascism Is a Lie" having appeared therein on June 22, 1937. In 1937 and 1938 he covered the Spanish Civil War for the North American Newspaper Alliance.

In 1927 Hemingway married Pauline Pfeiffer, a fashion writer, in Paris, France. The children, Patrick and Gregory, were born of this union and their custody was awarded to their mother at the time she secured an uncontested divorce from Hemingway several years ago. With reference to the first Mrs. Hemingway, it was reported that in June, 1940 that (the rest of the paragraph redacted, approximately 4 lines.)

(One complete paragraph redacted here, approximately 8–10 lines.)

(One paragraph redacted here, approximately 3–4½ lines.)

Hemingway allegedly has a passionate love affair with Martha Gellhorn which subsequently led to his divorce from his first wife. After the divorce Hemingway married Martha Gellhorn who is said to be a journalism in her own right and a contributor to Colliers magazine. In October, 1942, he was re-

–2–

portedly living with her on a farm near Havana, Cuba which had been purchased from Heger D'Ora. Martha Gellhorn apparently bought the farm before her marriage to Hemingway and after they married he moved there. Hemingway and Martha Gellhorn were in Spain at the same time during the Spanish Revolution as an article in the People's World for February, 14, 1939 indicated that a person recently back from Spain had remarked that he had met both Hemingway and Martha Gellhorn there.

Hemingway is still residing in Havana, Cuba and on December 7, 1942 was reportedly receiving his mail at the Ambos Mundos Hotel, Havana Cuba, and was said to be quite friendly with Manolo Asper, the manager of this hotel.

Hemingway was said to have a brother, Leicester Hemingway, who in April, 1942, was reported to be working for the Office for Emergency Management in Washington, D.C.

-3-

ACTIVITIES ON BEHALF OF LOYALIST SPAIN

During the Spanish Revolution Hemingway was very active in furthering the Loyalist cause and spent some time in Spain during this period. The Pearson and Allen column in the Sunday Mirror of January 17, 1937, contained the following remarks concerning Ernest Hemingway and the Spanish Revolution:

"Washington. — American sympathizers of the Spanish Red have been wasting a lot of good fighting.

"The left-wingers have been scrapping among themselves over who should rule the roost of a movement to aid the Red cause, almost as violently as the Reds in Madrid trenches have been battling to hold off General Franco and his horde of Moors and Fascist mercenaries.

"The story of this internecine feud is an amazing tale of petty factionalism and partisan intrigue.

"Last September, a group of prominent American liberals organized a non-partisan committee to help the Spanish government. Active in the movement were such notables as Ernest Hemingway, Suzanne La Follette, John Dos Passos and James Horty. A fund was started to send a fleet of twelve ambulances with a score of drivers to Spain.

"No sooner had the committee begun operating than factionalism threw a monkey wrench into the plan.

"It was discovered that of the twenty-one members of the committee, the Communists had quietly captured nineteen places. This embarrassed the original organizers, who had positively assured Spanish Ambassador de los Rios that the American aid would be free of politics.

"To offset this Communist coup, the Socialist organized a big mass meeting which they asked de los Rios to address.

"The Communists countered with a boycott of the affair. A free-of-all seemed in the making when cooler heads intervened and induced the rival parties to suspend hostilities and join in the meeting.

"Meanwhile, the ambulances, which it had been planned to rush to Spain in two weeks, were months getting under way."

The following information appeared in the column entitled "Lyon's den" by Leonard Lyons, in the January 26, 1937 issue of the New York Post:

"The report along Broadway last night was that Ernest Hemingway already had sailed for Madrid, and is now on the high seas, loyalist-bound ... To those who know him, this doesn't seem so strange. But to a million others there is wonder — as why a man who has fame, security and a family he loves should risk his life in war-torn areas .... What price Ideal? Yet this

-4-

isn't the first sacrifice Hemingway has made in pursuance of what he knows to be Truth. For years he's been rejecting invitations to got to Hollywood and write for the movies — at $4,500 a week. But during the past two weeks he allotted his time here to writing sub-titles, without pay or screen credit, for Akino films!"

While in Spain, during the Spanish Revolution, Hemingway was said to have associated with Jay Allen, of the North American Newspaper Alliance. It has been alleged by a number of sources that Allen was a Communist and he is known to have been affiliated with alleged Communist Front organizations.

He also was reportedly associated in Spain with Dr. Harman Frederick Erben. (One line and a fraction of a second line redacted here.) Dr. Erben, who was naturalized on January 29, 1941, in San Francisco, California, has stated that Hemingway was a friend of his with whom he fought during the Spanish Civil War.

Hemingway apparently spent sometime in a concentration camp in Spain.

A confidential informant who fought in the Spanish Civil War for the Loyalists, and who claimed to have been captured and placed in a concentration camp at San Pedros, Cardanas, Spain, stated that he met Ernest Hemingway while in this camp.

One Sam Baron, while testifying before the Dies Committee on November 23, 1938, read into the record the following article, which he stated had appeared in Walter Winchell's column, dated September 2, 1938, concerning Ernest Hemingway. This article and the testimony of Mr. Baron concerning Hemingway is as follows:

"Ernest Hemingway has a piece coming out in Ken about a correspondent for a powerful British newspaper. Because it would be libelous in England to mention the man's name it isn't. It tells how this correspondent tried to send out an uncensored story about Loyalist terrorism — that the soldiers are wantonly shot dead by their own fellows, etc. *** Hemingway tried to tell the newcomer that such terror happened last year — not anymore. — Nevertheless the man insisted on sending out the fabrication by a newspaper girl, who didn't know the contents of the sealed envelope. Had she been caught with it on her person, she would have been shot. — The newspaperman there finally intercepted the envelope and destroyed it.

"What I want to bring out here is that Ernest Hemingway, a courageous individual, whom I admire, and an able story teller, who had just gone to Spain, tried to talk upon political matters, which Ernest Hemingway does not understand, but has just been whitewashing Communist terror in Spain in the various articles he had written in the United States. He has here admitted that the Communists have been spreading terror in Spain and shooting their fellow loyalists in the backs."

-5-

According to the February 4, 1939 issue of The Daily Record, seventy-eight percent of America's leading writers released an appeal in February 3,1939 by Pearl Buck, Ernest Sutherland Bates and Ernest Hemingway, for the raising of the embargo which prevented the Spanish Republic from buying arms in the United States for its defense. An account of this also appeared in the Peoples' World on February 7, 1939.

On May 24, 1939, The Daily Worker carried an article entitled "Hemingway to Talk to Writer's Rally". This article stated that Ernest Hemingway, distinguished American writer, would make his first public appearance since his recent return from Spain, at the public meeting of the American Writer's Congress to be held at Carnegie Hall, Friday evening, June 4, that Hemingway, who had bought and equipped two ambulances for the Spanish Loyalists, reported the Civil War for a syndicate of American newspapers. According to this article, Earl Browder, General Secretary of the Communist Party, would also address this meeting on the problems of the intellectual and the people's front against Fascism.

A clipping reportedly from the New York Times of September 21, 1941, was furnished by a confidential source. This clipping announced that a dinner forum on Europe would be held October 9, at the Hotel Biltmore in New York, under the auspices of the American Committee to Save Refugees, the Exile Committee of the League of American Writers, and the United

American Spanish Aid Committee to raise funds for the transportation of anti-Fascist refugees from French concentration camps to the Americas. This clipping stated that Lillian Heilman and Ernest Hemingway were co-chairman of the dinner forum committee.

The above mentioned confidential source made the following remark concerning Lillian Heilman and Ernest Hemingway: "Lillian Heilman, who together with Ernest Hemingway is co-chairman, is an outright Communist. — Hemingway who is on the outs with the Communists, apparently is serving as an innocent friend." This source also made the allegation that the above mentioned organizations were "100% Communist controlled and run."

Abraham Lincoln Brigade

The New York Times of May 8, 1938 stated that Friends of the Abraham Lincoln Brigade, 125 West 45th Street, New York City put out a quarterly magazine known as "Among Friends." Hemingway was reported to be a contributor to this publication which was described as being devoted to the Loyalist cause in Spain and more particularly to the Abraham Lincoln Brigade.

The Daily Worker of February 3, 1939 indicated that Hemingway would speak on February 22, 1939 at a memorial meeting to be held in honor of the men who died fighting in the Abraham Lincoln Brigade.

The following article appeared in the February 11, 1939 issue of the Daily Worker:

-6-

"HEMINGWAY TO TALK AT SPAIN VET RALLY WED."

Stella Adler Opens (illegible) Day Drive;
Meetings Spur Spain Aid

"Ernest Hemingway will make his first public appearance in two years at a memorial meeting to honor all the Americans who died fighting for democracy in Spain. The meeting will be held Wednesday, Feb. 22, Washington's Birthday, at 8 p.m. at the Manhattan Center, 34th Street and Eighth Avenue under the auspices of the Friends of the Abraham Lincoln Brigade.

"In tribute to his splendid work in behalf of the American while he was in Spain, Hemingway will be escorted to the platform by a guard of honor composed of 40 veterans of the Lincoln Brigade. Hemingway personally purchased several ambulances which were assigned to the Lincoln Brigade.

"Our dead are a part of the earth in Spain now and the earth of Spain can never die," Hemingway explained. 'Each winter it will seem to die and each spring it will come again. Our dead will live with it forever …. And as long as all our dead live in the Spanish earth, and they will live as long as the earth lives, no system of tyranny ever will prevail.'

Along with Hemingway, Vincent Sheean will also deliver a eulogy to the men who died in Spain. Langdon W. Post will preside."

One Joseph Herth wrote a book, "Men in the Ranks" which purported to be the story of twelve Americans in Spain and which was published by the friends of the Abraham Lincoln Brigade in March 1939. Hemingway wrote a forward to this book.

In June, 1939, Hemingway's name was listed on the letterhead of the Abraham Lincoln Brigade as one of its sponsors.

The May 5, 1941 issue of The Daily Worker, Page 2, contained an article entitled "Vote Parley to Stress Fight for Peace Policy." This article reported a speech made by one John Gates a former Lieutenant Colonel, who fought in Spain, and credited Gates with making the following statement concerning Ernest Hemingway: "The war makers today," said Gates, "are actively using enemies who formerly worked with the movement for the Spanish Republic."

The speaker named such men as Louis Fischer, Ralph Bates, Vincent Sheean, and Ernest Hemingway. He referred especially to Fischer's autobiography which slanders the Spanish Communists and the Soviet Union, and Bates referred to speeches attacking the Communist Party. Bates also reportedly stated that the veterans of the Abraham Lincoln Brigade must "boldly expose the partial war policies of the Roosevelt administration."

-7-

An article appeared in the November 25, 1941 issue of the Daily Worker entitled "Hemingway Home, Calls Chamberlain 'Known War Fascist,' Decries Nazi Terror." This article announced that Hemingway had recently returned from Spain, and the Spanish Civil War, and stated that:

> "Hemingway characterizes the new pact between France and Germany 'shameful' and added 'I think there is no doubt that Chamberlain can be called the No. 2 Fascist of Europe. Hitler is still No. 1, but Chamberlain can easily be ranked in second place.'

> "The Loyalists are holding up splendidly against the combined armies of Hitler, Mussolini and France, the report stated. 'However, they are badly in need of food and supplies, and all democracies should come to their assistance.' ********** He had strong praise for the members of the Abraham Lincoln Battalion, and called several of them by their first names. 'However, the work of the International Brigade is done,' Hemingway said, 'the Loyalist army is now entirely Spanish, and what a wonderful military machine it is. Their courage is almost beyond belief.'"

A letterhead on the stationery of the Friends of the Abraham Lincoln Brigade Rehabilitation Fund, Inc. 109 North Dearborn Street, Room 408, Chicago, Illinois, listed the name of Ernest Hemingway as a sponsor for this organization. This letter was addressed to all "International Worker's Order Lodges", and requested that the various lodges raise at least $50 each to be used for hospitalization of wounded veterans who had returned to the United States.

American Rescue Ship Mission

An article appeared in the January 16, 1941 issue of The Daily Worker, entitled "Hemingway Reaffirms Backing of Rescue

Ship", which stated "Ernest Hemingway, noted American author who covered the war in Spain, tonight reaffirmed his vigorous support of the American Rescue Ship Mission it was announced at the national headquarters of the project, 200 5th Avenue, by Miss Helen R. Bryan, executive secretary.

"In a cable communication sent from Havana and addressed to Dr. Edward K. Barsky, National Chairman of the United American Spanish Aid Committee, the administering body of the mission, Mr. Hemingway praised the work of Dr. Barsky in Spain, and expressed the sincere hope that a ship would be obtained 'as soon as it is humanly possible to do so.'"

Both the American ship Rescue Mission and the United American Spanish Aid Committee were reported as having been Communist-controlled organizations.

An article appeared in the July 26, 1938 issue of The Daily Worker, official Communist Party organ, which listed Hemingway as one of the sponsors for the American Relief Ship for Spain.

-8-

Emergency Conference to Save Spanish Refugees

In December, 1941, it was alleged that Hemingway had been a sponsor of the Emergency Conference to Save Spanish Refugees, which at the time of the receipt of this information, was no longer in existence.

Joint Anti-Fascist Refugee Committee

Hemingway was listed in a memorandum received on August 27, 1942, from a confidential source as being a national sponsor for the Joint anti-Fascist Refugee Committee. This source made the following comment concerning the situation:

"On February 24, 1942 the American Committee to Save Refugees and the United American Spanish Aid Committee met in executive session and amalgamated to from the Joint Anti-Fascist Refugee Committee, hereinafter referred to as JAFRC. The purposes of the JAFRC are reported to be the returning to the United States of American members of the Loyalist Army of Spain who have been in prison or internment camps in Spain or France since the conclusion of the Spanish Civil War and to furnish a refuge for refugees from the present government of Spain. It seems to have broadened its aims to include the refugees of any of the countries of Europe which have been overrun by the Nazis. The original organizations were decidedly Communistic and were controlled by Communists for the benefit of Communists, extreme radicals and the Abraham Lincoln Brigade. It is believed that the present organization is of the same nature. It is reported that it has fifty active members."

Medical Bureau to Aid Spanish Democracy

A circular bearing the date of January, 1937 with the title "Medical Bureau to Aid Spanish democracy", and reportedly issued from 381 Fourth Avenue, New York City, stated that this organization had furnished eight hospitals, 113 nurses, and fifty-two ambulances, and that the writers, artists, screen and stage workers had been the most active in securing medical aid for the Spanish people, that during 1937, they had contributed about $10,000 to the medical bureau. This circular named Ernest Hemingway as having purchased two ambulances. Hemingway was also credited with the purchase of these two ambulances in a New York Times article on January 12, 1937. This article named Saul Carson, the executive Director of the Medical Bureau as its source of information. In a telegram to the Medical Bureau office in New York City, Hemingway had reportedly signified his intention of going to Spain soon.

On May 10, 1937, there appeared a large ad in the New York Times by the Medical Bureau which the ad itself described as being affiliated with the North American Committee to Aid Spanish Democracy. Hemingway was listed as one of the sponsors who had already helped them.

Motion Picture Artists Committee

The "News of the World," which was published by the Hollywood Anti-Nazi League and which has been described as "a journal in defense of American democracy" contained an

-9-

article on November 19, 1937 which listed Hemingway as one of the speakers for a huge "Christmas Drive for Spanish Children." This drive was reportedly sponsored by the Motion Picture Artists Committee.

North American Committee to Aid Spanish Democracy

H.L. Chaillaux, Director of the National Americanism Commission of the American Legion, while testifying before the Deis Committee on August 17, 1938, read into the record an article which appeared in the April 16, 1938 issue of The Daily Worker concerning the North American Committee to Aid Spanish Democracy.

The information from this article, as furnished by Mr. Chaillaux, is as follows:

"Following an appeal by Ernest Hemingway, Vincent Sheean and Louis Fischer for funds for ambulance to meet emergency conditions in Spain, $1,002 was received by the Washington chapter of the Medical Bureau and North American Committee to Aid Spanish Democracy, 381 Fourth Avenue, Dr. Herman F.

Reiseig, executive secretary announced yesterday.

"The telegram from Joel Berrall, of the Washington Friends of Spanish Democracy reads: 'In response to recent cable from Hemingway, Sheean and Fisher for ambulances, we are wiring herewith $1,002. We understand ambulances will be at the front within 3 days of receipt of the money in Paris. If time permits, the ambulance should be marked: 'Gift of the Federal employees of Washington, D.C., U.S.A.' Advise by wire today that this money has been cabled abroad.

Spanish Refugee Relief Campaign

Ernest Hemingway was listed as a sponsor on a letterhead of the Spanish Refugee Relief Committee dated April 19, 1939.

United Spanish Aid Committee

A circular was reportedly issued by the United Spanish Aid Committee, Room 554, Bradburg Building, 304 South Broadway, Los Angeles, California, having no date but bearing an address of Room 810-200 Fifth Avenue, New York City. This circular declared that the object of the above mentioned organization was to "help free men of the International Brigade in French and Spanish prison camps." A campaign for the release of the International Volunteers, 4,000 of whom were allegedly in French concentration camps. This circular listed Ernest Hemingway as one of the endorsers of the campaign to aid International Volunteers.

United Youth Committee to Aid Spanish Democracy

A report was received from a confidential informant who had covered a meeting of the United Youth Committee to Aid Spanish Democracy, held at the Shrine Auditorium in Los Angeles, California on February 24, 1937. According to this informant, approximately 4,000 persons attended this meeting which had been previously advertised by the Communist press and at organizational meetings. Donald Odgen Stewart presided at the meeting and lauded Ernest Hemingway for donating an ambulance to the Spanish Loyalists.

Writers and Artists Ambulance Corps

The Daily Worker of January 12, 1938 described Hemingway as one of the sponsors of the Writers and Artists Ambulance Corps which was said to have sent ambulances to Spain. Hemingway was also credited with having personally purchased the first two ambulances which were sent to that country in May, 1937.

Possible Connections with Communist Party

The following information was secured from a confidential source:

> "Ernest Hemingway, New York speciality writer for New Masses and Daily Worker, page 1, Daily Worker 9-13-35; wires greeting to Soviet Union, page 2, Daily Worker 5-2-38."

A former letterhead of the Deutsches Volksecho, which bore the date of February 16, 1939, carried the name of Ernest Hemingway as one of the contributors to this group.

In the fall of 1940 Hemingway's name was included in a group of names of individuals who were said to be engaged in Communist activities. These individuals were reported to occupy positions on the 'intellectual front and were said to render valuable service to propagandists. According to the informant, those whose names were included on this list loaned their efforts politically as writers, artists and speakers and traveled throughout the country supporting and taking part in Communist front meetings and in the program of the Party generally. They were alleged to be particularly active in the then paramount Communist Party objective, namely, defeat of the preparedness program.

Hemingway, according to a confidential source who furnished information on October 4, 1941, was one of the "heads" of the Committee for Medical Aid to the Soviet Union. This informant alleged that the above- mentioned committee was backed by the Communist Party.

(One paragraph redacted here, approximately three and a half-lines.)

Dr. Alfred Kantorowicz listed Hemingway as a reference at the time he filled out his alien registration from. Kantorowicz is a German alien and has been reported to be one of the chief liaison men between the German Communists in Mexico and the German Communists in the United States. He was also allegedly the founder of the League of German Writers in Exile in Paris, France.

In January, 1942 it was reported that the American Russian Cultural Association, Inc., of New York City, put out a small pamphlet soliciting support. The name of Ernest Hemingway appeared therein as a member of the Board of Honorary Advisors.

This group was purportedly organized to foster better relations between the United States and Russia.

A confidential informant reported on September 23, 1941 that Ernest Hemingway had broken all ties with the Communists.

-12-

MISCELLANEOUS ACTIVITIES

American Committee for the Protection of Foreign-Born

In January, 1940, Hemingway addressed letters over his personal signature endorsing the work of the American Committee for the Protection of Foreign-Born and soliciting the assistance of various persons. He requested that any contributions in the form of checks by made payable to him.

A confidential source furnished a memorandum dated October 18, 1941, concerning the American Committee for the Protection of Foreign-Born. This memorandum states that on March 2 and 3, 1940, the above-mentioned organization held its Fourth Annual Conference in Washington, D.C. and disseminated a circular soliciting sponsors. According to this memorandum, the circular contained a printed picture of the head and left arm of the Statue of Liberty, and opposed "registration and fingerprinting of non-citizens", which was regarded as a discrimination against the foreign-born. This circular was signed jointly by Ernest Hemingway and Dr. William Allen Neilson, as co-chairman for the Committee of sponsors.

A list of the sponsors of the American Committee for the Protection of Foreign-Born, 79-5th Avenue New York City, which was dated August 1940 contains the name of Ernest Hemingway.

According to a confidential source Hemingway and one Dr. William A. Neilson, who were co-chairman of the Committee of sponsors for the Fourth Annual Conference of this organization, wrote to the Editor of the People's World, an alleged Communist newspaper at San Francisco, seeking financial support for the committee in its drive against anti-alien bills then pending in Congress.

The Daily Worker of January 2, 1941, stated that Carey Williams, the California Commissioner of Immigration and Housing; Professor Walter Reutenstrauch, Dean of the School of Mechanical Engineering at Columbia University, and Dr. Max Yergan, President of the National Negro Congress, had accepted invitations to serve as co-chairman of the 1590 sponsors for the Fifth National Conference of the American Committee for the Protection of Foreign-Born to be held in Atlantic City on March 29 and 30, 1941. Hemingway was named as one of the sponsors of the Congress.

<u>American Writers Congress</u>

A circular advertising an "American Writers Congress" to be held at Carnegie Hall, New York City, on June 4, 1937, stated that Ernest Hemingway

-13-

and Earl Browder were to be speakers at this Congress. An account of this also appeared in the New York Times of May 24, 1937, which carried an article stating that Hemingway, who had spent some months in Spain, would make his first public talk on conditions there at the opening session of the National Congress of American Writers on June 4, 1937, at Carnegie Hall. Other speakers at this meeting, over which Archibald MacLeish presided, were speaker Gerald F. Nye, Earl Browder, Donald Odgen Stewart and Representative John P. Barnard. A confidential source commenting on this article stated that Hemingway was close to the Communist Party, but that he had no knowledge of Hemingway's actual membership in the Party.

An article appeared in the New York World Telegraph of June 5, 1941 entitled "Writer's Congress Held Communist

Cultural Front". This article was written by Frederick Woltman, a staff writer of the newspaper and stated, "The Fourth American Writers Congress opening tomorrow at the Commodore Hotel is part of a Communist cultural front which, since its origin six years ago, consistently has followed the political deviations of the Soviet Union and the Communist Party, a survey by the World Telegraph showed today."

This article goes on to state that the Writers Congress had been supported by many prominent individuals who resigned from this organization when the Communist Party "scrapped collective security and went in for isolationism following the Hitler Stalin Pact." Listed among the persons who were no longer connected with the Writers Congress due to its alleged following of the Communist Party line, was the name Ernest Hemingway.

League of American Writers

On February 21, 1941, Hemingway was reported as being a vice-president and member of the Board of Directors for the League of American Writers, Inc., which is reportedly a Communist front organization.

A circular reportedly published by the National Board of the League of American Writers, Inc., carried the name of Ernest Hemingway as President of the National Board. This circular solicited financial aid for those individuals who had fought with the Loyalists in the Spanish Revolution, and stated that the attempt was being made to bring them to Mexico. It contained the following statement concerning the alleged need for those persons to be removed from a French concentration camp.

"This cry no longer comes from some twenty writers thanks to the $13,200 which was raised at a dinner we held on October 17 in cooperation with a committee of leading publishers. Passage to Mexico has been bought for these fortunate exiles. But at least 75 others are awaiting our help. It now costs $600.00 per person to get them safely out of France, to Mexico. While they wait in Lisbon for

-14-

their chance to board the over-crowded boats, they must live, they must have food, money, medicine. And they count on us, Democratic Americans, to bring them to the safety of the New World."

<u>Mexican Trip</u>

(Two separate paragraphs redacted here, approximately 8–12 lines, per paragraph, about a third-page total.)

<u>GENERAL INFORMATION</u>

On one occasion Hemingway wrote an article against war which appeared in Esquire magazine. This article was later incorporated in a pamphlet prepared by the American Youth Congress and one individual at least was arrested for distributing these on November 11, 1935, in Seattle, Washington.

According to the April 1939 Bulletin of (illegible) for Democracy, Ernest Hemingway was at that time a member of the Advisory Board of this group.

On an unspecified date Hemingway tried to contact French Ambassador Gaston Henri-Haye. The reason for his desire to contact the Ambassador is not known. Mrs. Hemingway also tried to contact the French Ambassador in December 18, 1940.

The next file is dated June 1, 1943, from the Legal Attache, Havana, to the FBI in Washington. The right side of the fifth paragraph is blurred by various FBI stamps; the lines should probably read: "... the charge that Hemingway is now..." and "He advocates in..."

OFFICE OF THE LEGAL ATTACHE

EMBASSY OF THE
UNITED STATES OF AMERICA
HAVANA, CUBA
June 1, 1943

Director
Federal Bureau of Investigation
Washington, D.C.

Re: Ernest Hemingway

Dear Sir;

The Havana Communist daily newspaper "Hoy" on April 25, 1943, carried an extensive attack against ERNEST HEMINGWAY, displayed under a four-column heavy title-line: "THE LAST POSITION OF THE TRAITOR HEMINGWAY."

This article, written by Raul Gonzales Tunon, labeled HEMINGWAY'S "For Whom the Bell Tolls" a book "so miserable, so slanderous, that it met with excellent reception among the Fascists, the Trotskyists and the Munichists."

It condemned Hemingway as one of the "war tourists" who went to Spain, "not to seek the popular and eternal Spain but to seek curious effeminate' queer characters." On his failure to find such characters in the Loyalist zone, the article says, he made friends with the most "delirious" adventurers infiltrated in the CNT (Confederacion Nacional de Trabajo) and with the individualists of the Trotyskyist group of the POUM (Partido Obrero Uniuficado Marxists).

"The attacks on Andre Marty…. constitutes a continuation of known slanders whose origin must be sought in the propaganda office of Dr. Goebbels," the article stated.

It continues with the charge that "Hemingway is now the champion of the race theory in reverse. He advocates in the United States a campaign for the sterilization of all Germans as a means of preserving peace. That is, he wants to make this a racial war against Germany. He shakes hands with Goebbels, who, trying to prevent the disaster of the German people, says that 'the skin of every German is at stake in this war'. This idea of Hemingway's is a Trotskyist idea at the service of Nazism."

The article closes with the statement: "Here is the literate Hemingway, author of a slanderous book which is a rehash of others of his, this time directed against the Communist party and against the Spanish people. Here is the portrait of the revolutionary tourist. His destiny will be the destiny of all traitors, of all provocateurs who maneuver openly or in cover against the Communist party, against the people, against history. And against good literature."

(Three separate paragraphs redacted here, approximately five or six lines each, totaling about one-third of a page.)

Very truly yours,
(name redacted)
CONF. INFT. S.I.S. #<u>396</u>

On June 13, a detailed 10-page memo is prepared in the FBI Washington offices and forwarded to D.M. Ladd. At the end of this memo, Edw. A. Tamm added a rebuttal in italic type.

Federal Bureau of Investigation
United States Department of Justice
Washington, D.C.

June 13, 1943

MEMORANDUM FOR MR. LADD

Re: Intelligence Activities of
Ernest Hemingway in Cuba

BACKGROUND

Mr. R. G. Leddy, Legal Attache in Havana, Cubs, submits information concerning the intelligence activities of Ernest Hemingway and his relations with the FBI.

DETAILS

Ernest Hemingway has resided almost continuously in Cuba at a small country estate at San Francisco de Paula, outside Havana, during the past two years. In this time he completed his latest book, a compilation of war stories, published in the fall of 1942.

Hemingway knows Cuba well and has lived on the island for various periods during the past 12 years. He is well known as a sportsman, engaging in deep sea fishing from his own fishing boat and maintaining a pigeon shooting range on his own property. He is a well known figure at jai alai matches and a back-slapping friend of the Basque jai alai players. In Havana he frequents the Floridita and Basque Bar, two famous spots where prominent Cubans and Americans gather at noon and in the evening.

During the current period of his residence in Cuba, Hemingway had no contact with the American Embassy until August, 1942. He did, however, cultivate the friendship of an American Consul on a personal basis before this date. An Embassy employee and friend of this Consul remarked to the Legal Attache that Hemingway's purpose appeared to have been some kind of an "in" with American authorities at a time when he was only interested in completing his book. In August, 1942, Hemingway was introduced to the American Ambassador Mr. Spruille Braden, and volunteered his service to engage in intelligence work. The Ambassador inquired of the Legal Attache whether Hemingway would be useful to investigate the Spanish Falange with the aid of Spanish Republican refuges known to him. The Ambassador said that he regarded Hemingway's experience in the Spanish Civil War and his long-time acquaintance with Spain and the Spanish people as giving him unique qualifications to investigate the Spanish Falange in Cuba, which the Ambassador regarded as an imminent danger.

-2-

The Ambassador's inquiry was taken up by Mr. Joyce, Second Secretary of the Embassy, whether Legal Attache and Mr. Joyce was advised that there were some question of the attitude of Mr. Hemingway to the FBI, with which organization he had presumably been requested to work. This question existed, Mr. Joyce was advised, because of Hemingway's action as a principle signer of the denunciation of the FBI in the Detroit Communist-Spanish enlistment case in 1940 and also because of Hemingway's remark on meeting the Legal Attache some weeks previously at which time he referred to the FBI as "the American Gestapo." Mr. Joyce volunteered to sound out Hemingway on his attitude toward the FBI, as casually as possible, and returned with the advise that Hemingway has paid no particular attention to the petition he signed in 1940 denouncing the FBI and could now hardly remember what it said; Hemingway told Mr. Joyce that people are always shoving petitions under his nose and like many famous people he is inclined to sign them on the request of a friend without full information as to their contents. Hemingway also dismissed the reference to the FBI as "the American Gestapo" as a mere jest.

The American Ambassador, nevertheless, decided to engage Mr. Hemingway's services under his own personal direction without any direct contact with the Legal Attache. Arrangements were made whereby copies of Hemingway's reports would be furnished to the Legal Attache in order that the latter might be advised of developments in investigations conducted into the Spanish Falange by Ernest Hemingway.

One full paragraph redacted here — approximately 12 lines, about one-third of a page.)

The organization which Hemingway gathered for this work was composed exclusively of Spanish Republican refugees in Cuba. Their identity was not disclosed in Hemingway's reports but they were designed by a number. They grew from an original force of four full-time operatives, alleged to be former members of the Spanish police force, and 12 part-time

-3-

undercover agents employed as barkeepers, waiters, etc. to a total number of 26 informants composed of six full-time operatives and 20 undercover informants. The organization was located not only in Havana but also at Matansas, Comaguey and Santiago de Cuba, all down the island. The expenses of the organization were paid from the special funds of the American Embassy at the direction of the Ambassador and came to total nearly a thousand dollars a month. It is not known whether the identity of Hemingway's informants were ever disclosed to the American Ambassador but it is the belief of the Legal Attache that their identity was known only to Hemingway.

Hemingway claimed to operate the organization with the

greatest possible discretion, having sub-chiefs who contact the actual investigators and in turn reported to him, thereby separating him from any direct contact with the investigative work. To prevent any police action, however, the Ambassador personally requested of General Benitez, a letter stating that Hemingway was known to him, General Benitez, and should receive every consideration. This is not an exact statement since the only contact between General Benitez and Hemingway has been through the letter from the American Ambassador making the above request.

(One major paragraph redacted here, approximately eight to ten lines; about a quarter of a page.)

In August, 1942, Hemingway suggested to the Ambassador that Gustavo Duran, a Spaniard employed by the American Government in Washington, be brought to Cuba to operate his organization during a 30-day absence of Hemingway on a government mission for the Naval Attache along the coast of Cuba. Hemingway stated that he knew Duran well during the Spanish Civil War at which time Duran was a corps commander in the Spanish Republican Army and successfully defended the Valencia Front against the Franco forces until further resistance was made impossible because of the collapse of other fronts. Hemingway described Duran as a "military and intelligence genius of the type like Napoleon that comes along once in a hundred years." He said that Duran, who had married an American girl in England after the Spanish war, spoke French, German, English and some

-4-

Russian; that he was pure Republican, not a Communist, and would get to the bottom of the Falange in short order. Hemingway said the Duran was wasting his time as an employee of the Division of Cultural Relations in the Department of State and should be brought to Cuba to direct Hemingway's intelligence organization at least for this limited period. It was learned by the Legal Attache that Duran was actually an employee of the Coordinator of Inter-American Affairs, for which reason it was pointed out by the Legal Attache to the Ambassador that Duran's assignment in connection with intelligence work in Cuba might raise jurisdictional questions in Washington. The Ambassador took the position that Duran would be working directly under the Embassy and in any event his assignment was only for a period of 30 days.

Mr. Duran arrived in Cuba early in November, 1942, and began working with Hemingway. His work has not been of the same sensational character as Hemingway's, as noted below, but has not been in any way different or distinct from the type of reports which Hemingway has submitted. These reports as mentioned above are of the type received by Bureau Field Divisions from voluntary complainants, being unspecific and unverified and showing no continuing investigation to establish a line of conduct or suspicious activities by the subject.

The only innovation introduced by Mr. Duran was an attempted partial coverage of public opinion in Cuba in relation to the war and the United States submitted in reports entitled "The Voice of the Street." These reports contain quotations from persons in cafes, bars and pool rooms and claim to set out the opinion of the people regarding developments in the war. They are, however, limited to the type of individual met in such places and, in the opinion of the Legal Attache, do not represent a fair cross section of general public opinion. Likewise, in the extent of their coverage, these reports have not given the opinions of sufficient persons to warrant the conclusion that they reflect the thoughts of even this general class of Cuban individuals.

The American Ambassador, however, has been highly

impressed with this type of information and on his return from a trip to Washington in December, 1942, remarked that the reports were very well thought of in the Department of State.

Although Hemingway's services were engaged to investigate the Spanish Falange in Cuba, he soon branched out to cover the entire field of intelligence.

After reading an article in the New York Times about a new type of oxygen-powered submarine used by the Germans, Hemingway instituted an investigation of the supply and distribution of oxygen and oxygen tanks in

-5-

Cuba. He immediately advised that "at last with this development we have come to the point after months of work where we are about to crack the submarine refueling problem." Shortly afterwards, his investigation was referred to the Legal Attache by the Embassy and a check was made on the supply and distribution of oxygen and oxygen tanks throughout Cuba with the result that the available supplies were well-accounted for. The Naval Attache also participated in this investigation. Nothing further was heard from Hemingway about the subject.

Hemingway's investigations began to show a marked hostility to the Cuban police and in a lesser degree to the FBI.

About a week before the visit of President Batista to Washington, Hemingway sent in a report, presumably prepared by him, alleging preparations by General Benitez to seize power in Cuba and make himself President during Batista's absence from the country. His report stated that Benitez had no such ideas until his own trip to Washington "which had been so successful." The report alleged that Benitez was training a large squadron of motor cycle police officers with patrol cars and that the police force was being trained daily with rifles as a military unit. The report said that it was Benitez's plan to take Cuba while Batista and the American Ambassador, the two strongest individuals in Cuba, were absent and that an investigation should be commenced at once to uncover the preparations of Benitez in securing fire arms and steel protection shields for the motor cycle and squad cars.

Mr. Joyce asked the Legal Attache to check on this report. The Legal Attache pointed out that no such preparations as Hemingway alleged were observed by FBI agents working in daily contact at Police headquarters and that the training of the Cuban Police force with rifles is a practice which has gone on for years inasmuch as the Cuban National Police is an integral part of the Cuban Army. The danger of alienating police cooperation by this type of report was also pointed out to Mr. Joyce inasmuch as, according to a well known maxim, "there are no secrets in Cuba."

In the case of Prince Camilo Ruspoli, Italian Fascist leader interned by the Cuban authorities but confined to a clinic because of illness, Hemingway reported that Ruspoli had paid off the Cuban Chief of Police, General Benitez, and was not really ill, and inferred that the Legal Attache had accepted the word of the police as to the guarding of Ruspoli at the clinic without any investigation. Through Mr. Joyce, Hemingway was requested by the Legal Attache to secure details as to the actual state of health of Ruspoli. He promised to do so through an undercover operative employed as a male nurse at the particular clinic where Ruspoli was confined. Nothing further was heard from Hemingway about this phase of the investigation.

-6-

In December 1942, however, Hemingway reported that Ruspoli had attended a public luncheon in honor of the new Spanish Charge d'Affairs, Peyalo Garcia Olay, at the Hotel

Nacional. His report greatly disturbed the Ambassador; there was an immediate check at the Hotel Nacional by the Legal Attache and no substantiation of the public luncheon or the presence of Ruspoli could be found either from the hotel management and employees or from two of the guests alleged to have been present. The Ambassador was so advised and later Hemingway wrote a memorandum asking that his source, a waiter at the hotel, not be "grilled" by the FBI as this would destroy his usefulness; he also asked to see our proofs regarding the absence of Prince Ruspoli from this public luncheon.

Hemingway reported sighting a contact with a submarine and the Spanish steamer SS Marques de Comillas at high noon on December 9, 1942, off the Cuban coast. Hemingway was ostensibly fishing with Winston Guest and four Spaniards as crew members, but actually was on a confidential mission for the Naval Attache. The report was referred to the Legal Attache, both by the Embassy and by the Naval Attache with the request for investigation. The Legal Attache's investigation consisted of interview with Cuban Police cooperation, of forty crew members and some fifty passengers of the vessel, most of the latter known anti-Fascists repatriated from Spain. None of the persons interviewed would admit sighting a submarine as Hemingway had, from his 35-foot launch. The negative results of this inquiry were reported. Thereupon Hemingway submitted a memorandum stating that it would be a tragedy if the submarine was carrying saboteurs possibly let off the steamship at this point on a mission to the United States and that the Legal Attache discounted Hemingway's report because it had not come from an FBI Agent, thereby permitting the saboteurs to land in the United States without advance notice.

January, 1943, Mr. Joyce of the Embassy asked the assistance of the Legal Attache in ascertaining the contents of a tightly wrapped box left by a person at the Bar Basque under conditions suggesting that the box contained espionage information. The box has been recovered from the Bar Basque by an operative of Hemingway. The Legal Attache made private arrangements for opening the box and returned the contents to Hemingway through Mr. Joyce. The box contained only a cheap edition of the "Life of St. Teresa." Hemingway was present and appeared irritated that noting more was produced and later told an Assistant Legal Attache that he was sure that we had withdrawn the vital material and had shown him something worthless. When this statement was challenged by the Assistant Legal attache, Hemingway jocularly said that he was only joking and that he thought something was very funny about the whole business of the box.

-7-

Hemingway's ill-disguised hostility toward the FBI became more evident in February, 1943 when the Ambassador received charges that Special Agent Knoblaugh, just assigned to the Embassy as Assistant Legal Attache, was a participant in the Franco movement in Spain and had acted as a paid Franco propagandist. The Ambassador declined to disclose the source of these charges when they were promptly challenged and proof demanded by the Legal Attache. The latter learned, however, positively that the charges were given to the Ambassador by Ernest Hemingway and Gustavo Duran, as ascertained from a highly reliable and confidential source within the Embassy. The charges centered about a book written by Special Agent Knoblaugh "Correspondent in Spain" upon his return from assignment as an Associated Press correspondent in Madrid in 1938, Hemingway knew Special Agent Knoblaugh at that time and was most friendly with him. He had met him in Havana immediately after Special Agent Knoblaugh's arrival.

Although ostensively friendly, Hemingway made no remark to Special Agent Knoblaugh concerning his book or to the Legal Attache but took his complaint directly to the Ambassador. The latter admitted that he had read only the first forty pages of the book and after originally requesting the Legal Attache to have Mr. Knoblaugh transferred to another position where the Spanish Falange was not to the acute problem which the Ambassador believed it to be in Cuba, the Ambassador dismissed the subject as "not as important as he had originally thought."

In personal relations Hemingway has maintained a surface show of friendship and interest with representatives of the FBI. Through statements he has made to reliable contacts of the Legal Attache, however, it is known that Hemingway and his assistant Gustavo Duran, have a low esteem for the work of the FBI which they consider to be methodical, unimaginative and performed by persons of comparative youth without experience in foreign countries and knowledge of international intrigue and politics. Both Hemingway and Duran, it is also known, have personal hostility to the FBI on an idealogical basis, especially Hemingway, as he considers the FBI anti- Liberal, pro-Fascist and dangerous as developing into an American Gestapo.

Although Hemingway's opinions coincide with those of some Communists in this regard, he has repeatedly asserted that he is anti-Communist and that he was as much opposed to the Communist influence in the Spanish war as he was to the Fascist.

As of April 1, 1943, however, Hemingway's activities as an undercover informant for the American Ambassador were terminated. This resulted from general dissatisfaction over the reports submitted and the strong position against these services taken by Mr. Albert (illegible) ufer, Commercial Counsellor of the Embassy and a highly respected State Department official. An additional factor in motivating the ambassador's action was the

-8-

inconsistency of continuing to employ an undercover organization operated by Hemingway at a time when the Ambassador was discouraging and restricting the employment of paid informants by the official attaches of the Embassy.

While the investigations of suspects as such is discontinued, the Ambassador has requested Mr. Gustavo Duran to continue to turn in reports on public opinion in Cuba as previously undertaken by him in "The Voice of the Street." The Ambassador made this request of Mr. Duran because he feels that these reports give him an "inside picture" of what people are thinking in Cuba which he did not get in any other way; further, on his trip to Washington in December, 1942, the Ambassador was informed at the Department of State that these reports are received with great interest and for this reason he is desirous of continuing to submit them to Washington. A force of two or three Spanish agents will continue to gather this material for Mr. Duran with expenses estimated at no more than $200.00 per month. Mr. Duran is now employed at the American Embassy at Havana on a personal basis as a member of the Auxiliary Foreign Service. His time is devoted to analyzing political comments and articles in the Cuban press and assisting the Ambassador in the preparation of speeches to be given in Spanish.

The Legal Attache has mentioned to the American Ambassador that FBI representatives are prepared to gather and submit reports or public opinion. The Ambassador has shown no desire to take advantage of the investigative service of the FBI in this field. The Legal Attache at Havana states that the Ambassador has always regarded the Hemingway organization as a pet project of his own and in continuing a minor phase of its work the Ambassador has given the Legal Attache the impression that he is unwilling, nor merely for Hemingway's sake, but his own, to order a complete dissolution of Hemingway's organization. Hemingway, however, is not directly operating "The Voice of the Street" investigations but has turned them over entirely to Mr. Gustavo Duran.

(Two separate paragraphs redacted here; each approximately six-eight lines long.)

-9-

(Two paragraphs redacted here, the first approximately 10–12 lines long, the second approximately 8–10 lines.)

Hemingway has made this clear in regard to the film production of his book "For Whom the Bell Tolls." He sold the movie rights to the book more than two years ago; the picture was filmed and has gone through several editing processes and according to Hemingway's latest information, a final revision of the picture and reshooting of many scenes has resulted in the removal of all of what he considers the vital parts of the story relating to the Spanish Civil War and reduced it to what he terms a mere "Graustark romance." Hemingway has vigorously asserted that he will soon go to Hollywood to find out who is responsible for this treatment of his book and when he finds out he will make an incident of it which will cause the person responsible to regret having ever interfered with the story itself. Hemingway believes that influences which he terms "Fascist" namely the Vatican and some elements in the United States Department of State have been most influential in taking the teeth out of his story.

Regarding Hemingway's position in Cuba, the Legal Attache advises that his prestige and following are very great. He enjoys the complete personal confidence of the American Ambassador and the Legal Attache has witnessed conferences where the Ambassador observed Hemingway's opinions as gospel and followed enthusiastically Hemingway's warning of the probable seizure of Cuba by a force of 20,000 Germans transported to the island in 1,000 submarines. A clique of celebrity-minded hero worshippers surround Hemingway wherever he goes, numbering such persons as Winston Guest, Lieutenant Tommy Shevlin (wealthy son of a famous Yale football player), Mrs. Kathleen Vanderbilt Arostegui and several Embassy officials. To them, Hemingway is a man of genius whose fame will be remembered with Tolstoy.

-10-

Hemingway claims great political influence and told an Assistant Legal Attache that the FBI had better get along with him because he carried a lot of weight in Washington. The principal political influence of Hemingway known to the Legal Attache is that Hemingway's wife, the former Martha Gellhorn, is a personal and literary friend of Mrs. Eleanor Roosevelt and has a standing invitation to stay at the White House when in Washington.

Hemingway is gathering material for a book at the present time. Although his intelligence activities have ended, he is on a special confidential assignment for the Naval Attache chasing submarines along the Cuban coast and keeping a careful observance on the movements of Spanish steamers which occasionally come to Cuba. This naval patrol work of Mr. Hemingway is regarded by him and the Naval Attache as extremely confidential (two lines and approximately one fourth of a third line redacted here.)

The Legal Attache at Havana expresses his belief that Hemingway is fundamentally hostile to the FBI and might readily endeavor at any time to cause trouble for us. Because of his peculiar nature, it is the belief of the Legal Attache that Hemingway would go to great lengths to embarrass the Bureau if an incident should arise. In view of his prestige as a literary man, accepted by large section of public opinion in matters not related to writing, it is the recommendation of the Legal Attache at Havana that great discretion be exercised in avoiding an incident with Ernest Hemingway.

Respectfully,

C. H. Carson

Addendum: 5-21-43—I do not concur with the conclusion reached in this memorandum. The Bureau has by careful and impartial investigation from time to time disproved practically all of the so-called Hemingway information. I don't care what his contacts are or what his background is — I see no reason why we should make any effort to avoid exposing him for the phony that he is. I don't think we should go to out of our way to do this but certainly if in the protection of the Bureau's interest it is necessary to meet him head-on, I don't think we should try to avoid such an issue. I am also in strong disagreement with the statement contained in the last paragraph on page 8 of this memorandum. Since our investigation has disproved all of Hemingway's alleged facts, I see no reason why, if and when we are asked by person entitled to a frank answer that we should fail to so state. I think it is preposterous to take the position that we should not speak disparagingly of his information "because it might be of some value in the future." Such a premise is basically unsound.

Edw. A. Tamm

FBI officials in Washington and Havana continue to wrestle with the Hemingway problem.

June 21, 1943

Memorandum for: MR. LADD

With regard to the attached memorandum which was prepared by Mr. Leddy, Legal Attache at Havana, Cuba, and with regard to Mr. Tamm's addendum thereof, I think it only fair to point out that the memorandum is probably misleading in so far as correctly or accurately expressing exactly what Mr. Leddy had in mind. In the first place I think that the report with regard to Leddy's dealing with Hemingway and Ambassador Braden in connection with Hemingway's organization more or less speaks for itself. Leddy has never at any time so far as we can tell at the Seat of Government shown the slightest inclination to sidestep any challenge with regard to Hemingway whenever he felt that Bureau interests were involved to the slightest extent. It will be recalled that Mr. Leddy immediately after Ambassador Braden made his arrangement whereby Hemingway would carry on investigations through his so-called informants for the Embassy, sought Bureau permission to approach Ambassador Braden and point out that this would constitute a violation of the Bureau's jurisdiction. It will be recalled that the Bureau did not authorize Agent Leddy to take such action. I do know, however, that upon every occasion where opportunity presented itself for Hemingway and the quality of his work and his informants to be discussed with Braden arise, Leddy unhesitatingly pointed out to Mr. Braden exactly what the true situation and facts were to the knowledge of Leddy.

During a conversation which I had with Robert Joyce, third Secretary of the Embassy at Havana, Joyce mentioned to me that Leddy, early in the stage of Hemingway's operations, convinced Joyce that the Hemingway setup was not propitious and was not altogether sound. Joyce is a professed personal friend of

Hemingway and of Braden. Joyce told me that Leddy handled this entire matter both with Joyce and Ambassador Braden in a scrupulously fair, impartial and direct manner. I believe it is quite pertinent to note that despite Ambassador Braden's and Joyce's protestations of friendship and admiration for Hemingway, the later is no longer in any way connected with the American Embassy in Havana, which fact is attributed to Leddy having furnished the true facts to Joyce and the Ambassador and also having utilized the opportunity of Ambassador Braden insisting upon knowing the identity of the Attache's informants by pointing out to the Ambassador the incongruity of having the Attache required to furnish the identity of informants and Hemingway not similarly required.

It should be further recalled that in connection with the matter involving Special Agent Knoblaugh in Havana, Leddy handled this in a very firm and uncompromising manner. He accepted the challenge and insisted that the Ambassador produce substantiation with regard to the allegations that Knoblaugh is a Falangist; this the Ambassador would not do; whereupon, Leddy together with Knoblaugh pointed our to the Ambassador information which would seem to completely explode any charges to the effect that Knobalugh is a Falangist. This caused Ambassador Braden in so far as his dealing with Leddy are concerned, to immediately back down with regard to his request that Knoblaugh be removed from Cuba.

With regard to the wording contained in the last paragraph of the memorandum on page 8, it is believed that this is somewhat unfortunate in setting out what Mr. Leddy actually hand in mind. It is known to the writer that Leddy has upon his own inclination whenever called upon to do so by the Ambassador and by Joyce, advised these two unhesitatingly that the information furnished by Hemingway and the latter's organization was completely unfounded and unsubstantiated in every single instance. Leddy, of course, accomplished this by furnishing the results of his, Leddy's, check as to the reports of Hemingway. I am quite sure that what he intended to express in the unfortunately worded paragraph is that he does not feel that information furnished by Hemingway should be ignored and disregarded as having come from unreliable sources solely because such information has in the past proved unsubstantiated. It is believed that he is also seeking to point out what is true with regard to conjecture, probabilities, and vaguely worded allegations that it is impossible to definitely establish that no truth whatsoever is contained in the allegations and information furnished. It is believed that Mr. Leddy will agree with the Bureau if inquiry should be made by persons entitled to know the truth, he respond by furnishing the exact facts in so far as information furnished to the office of the Legal Attache by Hemingway is concerned, that is that the information has been in no way verified or substantiated by investigation.

Respectfully,

C. H. Carson

The Legal Attache in Havana files another memo to the FBI in Washington, updating the Cuban press attacks on Hemingway.

OFFICE OF THE LEGAL ATTACHE

EMBASSY OF THE
UNITED STATES OF AMERICA
HAVANA, CUBA

June 26, 1943

Director,
Federal Bureau of Investigation
Washington, D.C.

Re: ERNEST HEMINGWAY —
INTELLIGENCE ACTIVITIES IN CUBA

Dear Sir;

As of general interest to the Bureau, the following matters affecting general intelligence activities are set forth.

1). <u>Communist Attack on Ernest Hemingway</u>

SIS #360 submitted a memorandum concerning the attack in the Communist newspaper "Hoy" of April 25, 1943, against Ernest Hemingway. The article is entitled, "The Last Position of the Traitor Hemingway," and is written by Raul Gonzales Tunon.

The article attacks Hemingway on several grounds. First, it condemns him as being one of the "war tourists" who went to Spain, not to seek the popular and eternal Spain, but to seek curious, "effeminate" queer characters. Not finding such characters in the Loyalist zone, they made friends with the most "delirious" adventurers infiltrated in the CNT and with the individuals of the Trotskyist group of the POUM. On Hemingway's return to America, he published a book that was "so miserable, so slanderous", that it met with excellent reception among the Fascists, the Trotskyists and the Munichists. This was "For Whom the Bell Tolls." The attack on Andre Marty ... constitute a repetition of known slanders whose origin must be sought the propaganda office of Dr. Goebbels."

Now, the article states Hemingway is a champion of race theory in reverse. He advocates in the United States a campaign for the sterilization of all Germans as a means of preserving peace. That is, he wants to make this a racial war against Germany. He shakes hands with Goebbels, who, trying to prevent the disaster of the German people, says that "the skin of every German is at stake in this war." This idea of Hemingway's is a Trotskyist idea at the service of Nazism.

The article closes stating "Here is the literate Hemingway, author of a slanderous book which is a rehashing of others of his, this time directed against the Communist Party and against the Spanish people. Here is the portrait of the revolutionary tourist. His destiny will be the destiny of all traitors, of all provocateurs who maneuver openly or in cover against the Communist Party, against the people, against history. And against good literature."

The original of the above article is retained in the files of this office since the above sets forth a complete and adequate summary.

2). <u>Intelligence activities of Mr. Hemingway</u>

It is learned that at the present time, Hemingway is continuing a project of (approximately one and three-fourths lines redacted here) involving a check of coastal water off northern Cuba for the possibility of enemy submarine or clandestine radio activity. (Approximately three and one-third lines redacted here, to the end of the paragraph.)

Although the Hemingway land intelligence organization was shut down by the Ambassador on April 1, 1943, this office continues from time to time to receive copies of memoranda submitted to Mr. Hemingway's assistant, Mr. Gustavo Duran, who is now employed at the American Embassy as a member of the Auxiliary Foreign Service. These memoranda are few in number and relate to cases which were previously under investigation. Mr. Duran has stated that they are submitted to him by the former operatives of the Hemingway organization on a voluntary basis. It is nevertheless known to the writer that Hemingway personally had 122 gallons of gasoline charged to him from the embassy's private gasoline allotment, for the month of April, 1945. When the Hemingway organization was functioning, arrangements were made that gasoline necessary for transportation in connection with the intelligence work would be allotted from the Embassy's private stock, which is apart from and not subject to Cuban rationing restrictions.

Mrs. Hemingway, the former Martha Gellhorn, a writer from Colliers, recently solicited from Mr. R. P. Joyce, Second Secretary of Embassy, information concerning conditions on the island or Martinique, with special reference to American-French relations in regard to the "blockade" of Martinique. She sought this information in order to complete a book setting forth results on a cruise in the Caribbean waters which she took in the fall of 1942. Mr. Joyce obtained the information from Mr. James Bonbright, who is handing the French desk in the Department of State.

3). <u>Relations with Bureau Informants</u>

(One major paragraph redacted here, approximately one fourth of a page.)

On the other hand, Mr. Hemingway entertained Secretary of the Treasury Henry Morgenthau at his finca during the visit of this official to Havana in March of this year. Since that time, correspondence has passes from the Secretary of the Treasury to Mr. Hemingway through the State Department diplomatic pouch.

Very truly yours,
#396
Legal Attache

The Legal Attache files another memorandum to the FBI in Washington, about Hemingway's book-in-progress. The end of the first paragraph of this memo is instructive for what the FBI thinks of Hemingway and how the Bureau imagines itself. The line CONFD. INFT. S.I.S. #396 was apparently stamped in, later.

Director,
Federal Bureau of Investigation
Washington, D.C.

Re: ERNEST HEMINGWAY

Dear Sir;

SIS # 357 advises that Mr. Hemingway, of whose intelligence activities under Ambassador Spruille Braden the Bureau has been previously advised, is currently engaged in writing a book based on his experiences in that work. Hemingway states that all of the people whom he has known during the last year in Cuba in connection with the intelligence work will appear in his book, including Ambassador Braden. We are not yet informed as to what role the representatives of the FBI will play, but in view of Hemingway's well known sentiments, will probably be portrayed as the dull, heavy-footed unimaginative professional policeman type.

(One full paragraph redacted here approximately six to seven lines.)

Very truly yours,

[CONF. INFT. S.I.S. #396]

R.G. Leddy

Legal Attache

Leddy again files a lengthy memorandum. It is unclear whether this was sent to the FBI in Washington.

Havana, Cuba
August 13, 1943

MEMORANDUM:

RE: GUSTAVO DURAN
Confidential Embassy Matter

Gutavo Duran came to Cuba on November 12, 1942. He was then in the employee of the Office of the Coordinator of Inter-American Affairs. His trip to Cuba was requested by the American Ambassador, the Honorable Spruille Braden, in order to engage the intelligence work under the Ambassador's direction. The Ambassador was then operating an undercover intelligence organization, directed by Ernest Hemingway, for the special purpose of securing information on Spanish Falange activities. Duran was recommended to the Ambassador by Hemingway, who described him as the ideal man to conduct this work, "an intelligence and military genius that comes along once in a hundred years." Originally intending to remain here on thirty days' special leave from the Coordinating Committee, Gustavo Duran was, through the Ambassador's influence, taken into the Embassy as a member of the Auxiliary Foreign Service early in January, 1943.

Ernest Hemingway, who was in Spain during the Spanish Civil War, knew Duran at that time; he is mentioned in Hemingway's "For Who the Bell Tolls," and was active with the Spanish Republican troops, finally attaining the rank of Lieutenant Colonel and being in command of the Army Corps defending Valencia at the end of the war.

(One complete paragraph redacted here, approximately six to eight lines.)

Gustavo Duran is the son of a Spanish General of the same name, who in his time enjoyed a high reputation as a military man. Duran received a good education and has I (illegible) foundation, but he never obtained any academic degree because he quit school to pursue his theatrical abilities. Although they seem to have been all-consuming, he never reached the prominence he desired. He spent some time in studying the theater, however, and went to Hollywood where he was given trials before the camera.

He was known politically in Madrid as a fervent Communist, militant in the party in which he held various high positions of authority and representation. When the Civil War broke out, he joined voluntarily the Communist militia, and was assigned to a command in the forces under Colonel MANGADA on the Madrid front. He spent the best part of the war on this front, ascending, always with the aid and support of the Communist

Party, in military rank until he reached the rank of Commander, before 1938. In the latter year, he was promoted to the rank of Lieutenant Colonel — highest rank granted by Republican Spain to non-professional officials — and served as chief of staff of an army corps on the Matallana (Valencia) front.

Close friends who served with and under him have highly praised his military conduct. He was known as a brave soldier and intelligent leader, although always seeming to work for political rather than military ends.

In the last days of the war, when Catalonia had already been occupied by the Francoites, a National defense Junta consisting of General MAIJA, BSTEREIRO, Colonel CASADO and others was formed to negotiate the surrender of Madrid with Franco. The Communist Party violently opposed this plan, arising in arms against the Junta. Orders were given to all comrades to march against Madrid and over throw the Junta.

The military chieftain of the CNT (Anarchist Labor Union of Syndicalists), CIPRIANO MERA, allied himself with the Junta, and one of the bloodiest battles of the war resulted, the Communists on one side and the Republican and CNT on the other.

Duran, on this occasion, obediently followed the party call, deserting his assigned post and leading the forces under him against the Republican and CNT in Madrid. He took a leading role in the fight, which however ended in defeat for his men.

He fled Spain via the port of Gandia, Valencia, on a British destroyer. By coincidence, on the same boat was Colonel Casado, against whom he had fought in Madrid. So well known was the enmity between those two that they were kept separated and under watch during the trip to France lest they stage an incident on board ship. From France he was able, by virtue of having a

North American wife, to go to England and hence to the United States and Cuba, where he is now stationed.

The statements of persons who knew him well in Spain and who fought with him are unanimous in that Duran is a product of the Communist school, and follows the code — "the end justifies the means." They say he can adapt himself to any situation which may be ultimately beneficial to the political beliefs with which he is so firmly imbued.

He has become a naturalized American citizen, and pretends to conform absolutely with the ideals of American democracy, but those who know him state that they do not believe him when he talks this way. They believe that he is merely using these tactics of his own ends, and that he cannot divorce himself from the beliefs which he has defended so many years during his life. Others state that the Communists frequently boast they have within the American Embassy now a man who is absolutely trustworthy as a source of information for them. It would not be surprising to many who knew Duran if the person referred to was this man.

In an effort to secure some independent corroboration of the above report, at the instruction of SIS # 396 further investigation was had by SIS # 788 with Dr. JUAN CHABAS, a Spanish refugee now in Cuba. A report of this conversation follows:

The writer last night had dinner with Dr. Juan Chabas, 75-year old Spaniard who prior to the Spanish Civil War was Juvenile Court Judge in Madrid. Although the old gentleman was not active in politics himself, his son JUAN CHABAS MARTIN, was a Lieutenant Colonel in the Spanish Loyalist Army, and for this reason the father fled Madrid on November 7, 1936, when it looked like Franco was going to enter the city at any moment. The elder Chabas went to France and then came to Santo Domingo with a group of Spanish refugees, finally reaching Cuba, where he has settled at Cienfuegos.

During the evening, events which took place in Madrid during the war days were discussed. The old man frankly stated that his son, now also a resident of Cuba, had been linked with the Communists in Madrid. Since coming to Cuba, the son has been doing various bits of work for the Casa de la Cultura in Habana, the father said.

The writer asked the old man if he had happened to meet Gustavo Duran in Madrid. Chabas said that he had, and that his son had been a very close friend of Duran. Duran and the son had fought together in Spain during the war, the father stated. The writer asked whether this meant that Duran was also a member of the Communist Party in Spain. Chabas said: "Yes, Gustavo became a Communist. But he was not actually a member of the party at the beginning of the war as far as I know. He had many friends among the Communists and had worked with them, but it was not until after the war had been going on a while that he joined the party."

When informed that Duran now is in Habana, the old man was quite surprised. He said that his son had told him Duran had come to America, but he did not know that he was here. He then changed the subject to painting, at which he now makes his living. He is residing in Cienfuegos, but had come to Habana to see about an exposition. The above conversation took place in the presence of JESUS PERNAS, of Pernas y Cia. Habana.

(The rest of the page redacted and an additional two pages omitted from the file. Two lines at the top of the page following the omitted material also redacted.)

In order to check on the accuracy of the foregoing statements, informal interview was had with Gustavo Duran by SIS #498 on July 30, without of course disclosing in any way the purpose of the conversation. The complete memorandum submitted by SIS #498 is set out as follows:

When questioned regarding the strength of the Communist Party in Spain at the outset of the Spanish Civil war and why Spaniards embraced the Communist cause, he stated that the Party in 1936 is reputed to have had 30,000 members in Spain, although he doubted that more than half this number were actually registered members, the other half being Communist sympathizers. He emphasized the fact that a great many ardent Republican Spaniards who believed in Spain had embraced the Communist cause since the Russians were the only ones furnishing aid to the Republican forces. He pointed out that although the Russians did not say so in so many words, it was apparent that they wanted the Communist Party members to pilot their planes and handle the materials they furnished. Russians officials were, of course, sprinkled throughout the Republican forces to see that this policy was carried out. Therefore, many Republicans joined the Communist Party in order to best serve their country.

He observed that had the Fascists, for example, furnished planes, munitions, and other war equipment to the Republican forces, these same Spaniards in the interest of the cause for which they were fighting would have become fascists under the same circumstances. However, as the war went on, Republican forces found that the equipment furnished by the Russians was obsolete, outmoded, and almost invariably old. As an example, he mentioned field artillery equipment furnished by the Russians which he identified as having been used by the Russians during the Russo-Japanese war in 1905. As a result of this half-hearted support by the Russians, many of the so-called Communists lost interest and enthusiasm for the cause. He also pointed out that following the defeat, a great many former "Communists" dropped their membership and affiliation with the Party. To summarize, he emphasized that many Spanish Communists joined the party simply as a matter of expediency in order to best utilize the aid furnished by the Russians.

Duran stated that he was last in Madrid in June, 1938, at which time he received his assignment to the Valencia sector, where he was in command until the end of the war, never having returned to Madrid. He mentioned that MIAJA was in charge of the defense of Madrid while Col. CASADO was in charge at Andalucia holding a similar position as Duran at Valencia.

Regarding the alleged difficulty between certain Republican officers and the Communists with respect to the surrender of Madrid, he stated that he only heard that there was difference of opinion on this point, but was unaware that any actual violence took place between the two factions. He emphasized that since he never returned to Madrid, facts as to what took place there are unknown to him.

Following an unsuccessful offensive at Teruel made by Duran, his forces retired to Valencia, and military operations were rather quiet from then until April 28, 1939, at which time he received orders to cease firing. On the following day, he received orders to proceed to a certain prisoners camp with his men, but they were stopped a short distance from Valencia and ordered to return to the city. He pointed out that the Franco government had made no provisions or plans whatsoever for prison camps, and guards were therefore placed around the city of Valencia and the Republican troops were allowed to move freely within the city.

Prior to the surrender of Madrid, Duran had been contacted by STUART WARNER, American Counsul and Col. FUQUA, American Military Attache, as well as a Mr. BALLANTYNE, British Vice Consul, and the British Military Attache. These men had contacted him for military information, ad he had become particularly friendly with Ballantyne. Following the surrender, Duran requested Warner to give him asylum in the American Embassy. Warner pointed out that the American government had not recognized the right of asylum, and therefore his request could not be granted. Duran also requested that he be permitted to live in his, Warner's home. Warner also refused this request. In desperation, Duran finally decided to present himself to the military commander of Valencia, which he did. He found this individual to be an old friend of his family. He ordered Duran billeted in a private home awaiting decision as to what action if any would be taken against him. While there, he wrote to Warner requesting him to telephone Ballantyne at the British Embassy, which was done. Ballantyne contacted Duran clandestinely, and advised him that a British destroyer was leaving from the port of Valencia that same night, and he could endeavor to get him on it. After considerable maneuvering, Duran was taken in an Embassy car to the British Embassy, and subsequently without passport or documents, posed as a British subject and succeeded in getting on board the vessel. Ballantyne also furnished him funds. The destroyer left Valencia, and Duran was later transferred from the British ship "Maine", which took him to Marseilles, France. From Marseilles, he took a through train to Dieppe on the channel. From Dieppe he crossed to London, and there was received by a British relief organization for Spanish refugees.

He is very grateful for the aid given him by the British in Valencia, which he believes saved his life or at least many years in prison.

During the course of his conversation, he mentioned that he had never been to the United States prior to his marriage to his American wife. He also mentioned that he studied literature, music and art in Madrid and Paris, although was unable to finish these studies on account of the civil war.

While discussing the Communists in Spain and the part they played in the war, Duran constantly referred to them as "they", and never gave any indication he personally was member of the Communist Party.

The following conclusions are noted:

(One full paragraph redacted here, approximately eight to ten lines.)

2) Gustavo Duran (about two-thirds of a line redacted here) was once in Hollywood and received a screen test. According to his own statement, he was never in the United States prior to 1940.

3) Before the close of the war in Spain in April, 1939 (a part of the line and half the next line redacted) Gustavo Duran went to Madrid to oppose with the Communists the surrender of the city to Franco. According to his own statement, he never returned to Madrid after June 1938. The statement of Duran that he was unaware of any violence between the two factions at Madrid appears inconsistent with widespread information, printed in the press of the world at that time concerning disorders in Madrid over the Communist refusal to join with other Spanish Republican elements in the final surrender of the city.

4) (The first one-third of this line redacted) mention that Gustavo Duran was able to go to England from France, having an American wife. It is known definitely from conversations, clippings, photos, etc. which Duran has shown, that he met his wife, who is American, in England after arrival there from France in 1939. In this detail, the original information appears inaccurate.

5) One paragraph redacted here, about five lines. Second full paragraph redacted, approximately eight lines. Third full paragraph redacted here, approximately eight to ten lines.

    c) Through (c & d) a check of newspapers, periodicals, and other publications in Loyalist territory between July 1935 and April 1939. In the event that Gustavo Duran was as active in Community Party affairs as it reported, it is almost certain that there will be a documentary record of his activities in the files of such publications. It is not known here where such files may exist; it is possible that such institutions as the Library of Congress, the library of the Workers' University at Mexico City, the archives of the New York "Daily Worker", or the offices of such Spanish Republican organizations as the JARE (Junta de Auxilio a los Refugiados Espanoles) in Mexico City, may have files of such publications.

    d) Check could be made of the records of MID, War Department, for any information on Duran reported by Col. Stephen A. Fuqua, then Military Attache at Madrid.

Among other duties, Mr. Duran reviews the local press for the Ambassador, and prepares speeches and lectures for the Ambassador in Spanish. The Ambassador has a high regard for his abilities. This, coupled with the fact that the Ambassador brought Mr. Duran into the Embassy on his own initiative, creates a problem for handing this matter which the writer desires to refer to the Bureau.

In addition, the close relationship between Duran and Ernest Hemingway is emphasized, and the Bureau is advised that we may well expect a violent attack from Hemingway if a report concerning Communist Party membership on the part of Gustavo

Duran becomes known to him. In spite of the termination of his intelligence organization on April 1, 1943, Hemingway's influence with the Ambassador appears unchanged.

Very truly yours,
[CONF. INFT. S.I.S. # <u>326</u>]
Legal Attache

Same date — Leddy files a memorandum to J. Edgar Hoover about Hemingway's book-in-progress. It is a near-duplicate of Leddy's previous memo about Hemingway's book, with the same date. It may have been filed to identify S.I.S. agent 357, as John Kelly. The name is hand-written above the beginning of the first line: S.I.S. #357.

OFFICE OF THE LEGAL ATTACHE

EMBASSY OF THE
UNITED STATES OF AMERICA
HAVANA, CUBA

August 13, 1943

Director,
Federal Bureau of Investigation
Washington, D.C.

Re: ERNEST HEMINGWAY

Dear Sir;

John Kelly
SIS #357 advises that Mr. Ernest Hemingway of whose intelligence activities under Ambassador Spruille Braden the Bureau has been previously advised, is currently engaged in

writing a book based on his experiences in that work. Hemingway states that all of the people who he has known during the last year in Cuba in connection with intelligence work will appear in his book, including Ambassador Braden. We are not yet informed as to what role the representatives of the FBI will play, but in view of Hemingway's known sentiments, will probably be portrayed as the dull, heavy-footed unimaginative professional policeman type.

(One full paragraph redacted here, approximately eight-ten lines.)

Very truly yours,

R.G. Leddy

Legal Attache

FBI administrator C. H. Carson prepares a memorandum for D. M. Ladd. Underlines appears to have been made in pencil. Someone else — perhaps Ladd — added a note under the end of the memorandum. It does not appear to be in Carson's handwriting. A script initial under the added note is illegible.

FEDERAL BUREAU OF INVESTIGATION
DATE <u>AUGUST 21, 1943</u>
MEMORANDUM FOR MR. LADD
Re: Ernest Hemingway, Cuba

<u>BACKGROUND</u>

The following information is of interest in connection with the activities of Ernest Hemingway in Cuba and his attitude toward the Bureau representatives in that country. <u>Information

<u>concerning the complete extent of Hemingway's intelligence activities under the personal direction of the Ambassador in Cuba has been previously brought to your attention.</u>

DETAILS

Recently, Ernest Hemingway advised a Bureau undercover representative in Cuba concerning a book which Hemingway is currently writing, based on his experiences in intelligence activities under the American Ambassador. Hemingway stated that all of the people whom he has dealt with during the past year in Cuba in intelligence matters will be mentioned in the book, including Ambassador Braden. In this connection the Bureau legal attache at Havana states that no information has been received as to what extent FBI representatives will be mentioned in the book.

However, Hemingway's attitude toward the FBI is already known, as indicated by Hemingway's action in signing a petition castigating the Bureau in connection with the Detroit Spanish Enlistment Case in 1940, and more recently indicated in Hemingway's remark that the FBI is "the American Gestapo". (One full paragraph redacted here, approximately six lines.)

ACTION

No action is recommended in this matter at the present time, and the above information is being set out to supplement information previously called to your attention concerning Ernest Hemingway.

Respectfully,

C.H. Carson

We ought to try
+ keep close to this
development

D.M. Ladd prepared a lengthy profile on Gustavo Duran, to be forwarded to J. Edgar Hoover.

Federal Bureau of Investigation
United States Department of Justice
Washington, D.C.

August 28, 1943

MEMORANDUM FOR THE DIRECTOR

Re: Gustavo Duran
Possible Community Party In-
Filtration into American Embassy
Havana, Cuba

(One major paragraph deleted here, approximately 12–14 lines.)

DETAILS

[PERSONAL HISTORY INFORMATION CONCERNING GUSTAVO DURAN]

Background Information

An employee investigation conducted by the Bureau for the Office of Emergency Management disclosed that Gustavo Duran was born on November 14, 1906 in Barcelona, Spain. Duran was brought up and educated in Madrid, Spain and in the Canary Islands. He studied piano at the Conservatory of Madrid, and composed a ballet for orchestra to be performed by the dancer Madam Argentina, which was performed throughout Europe in 1927. From 1929 to 1934, Duran lived in Paris where he furthered his musical studies and devoted himself to composition of musical works. In 1934, Duran began employment with Fono Espana Studios, Incorporated, as an adviser for the Latin American productions of that company. From 1936 to 1937, Duran has stated he supported the Constitutional Government of Spain, and after enlisting as a private in the Republican Army was eventually promoted to command of the Twentieth Army Corps, where he served in the Spanish Civil war. Duran escaped from Spain following a victory of the Franco forces, and resided in England from April 1939 to May, 1940, during which time he resumed his musical studies.

On December, 4, 1939 at Totnas, England, Duran married Bonte Romilly Crompton, an American citizen.

Gustavo Duran departed from Liverpool, England, and entered the United States at New York City on May 28, 1940. He became a naturalized citizen of the United States on November 3, 1942.

Employment Record

From August, 1939, to May, 1940, Duran was employed in London, England, by the Film Center, where he supervised Spanish and Portuguese versions of technical films distributed by the Film Center in the Western Hemisphere.

From March until October, 1941, Duran was employed by the Museum of Modern Art in New York City arranging musical scores for technical and educational films selected by the Office of Coordinator of Inter-American Affairs for distribution to other American Republics.

From November, 1941 to September, 1942, Duran was employed by the Music Division of the Pan American Union in Washington, D.C., where he was engaged in research and organization of musical projects at a final salary of $4,600. per annum. In this capacity, Duran served as Liaison Officer between the Pan American Union, the Office of Coordinator of Inter- American affairs and the State Department. In November, 1942, Duran went to Havana, Cuba, where he was given a position in the American Embassy after Ernest Hemingway had prevailed upon the American Ambassador to utilize the services of Duran in connection with Intelligence activities in Cuba for a temporary period. At the present time, Duran is assigned to the American Embassy in Havana as a member of the Auxiliary Foreign Service, Among his other duties, Duran reviews local newspaper articles for the Ambassador, and prepares speeches and letters in the Spanish language for the Ambassador, who has a high regard for Duran's abilities.

Military Career

Gustavo Duran enlisted in the Spanish Loyalist Army as a private on July 17, 1936, after which he distinguished himself in action, and reportedly rose to the rank of Acting General in command of an army corps.

Ernest Hemingway, who knew Duran in Spain and who mentioned him in his book "For Whom the Bells Tolls," has described Duran as a military genius, that "comes along once in a hundred years."

Duran was assigned to a command in the forces under Colonel Mandaga on the Madrid front, and by 1936, he had reached the rank of commander in the Loyalist forces. Duran was transferred to the Valencia front in 1938, and was promoted to the rank of Lieutenant Colonel, the highest rank granted by Republican Spain to non-professional officers, and he served as Chief of an army corps with considerable success.

(One third of a line and several words written in above the line are redacted here) has stated that in the last days of the Civil War in 1939, when Catalonia had been occupied by Franco

Forces, a National defense Junta was formed under General Miaja to negotiate the surrender of Madrid with General Franco. In it reported the Communist Party violently opposed this plan, and orders were given to all comrades to march against Madrid and overthrow the Junta. This source states that Cipriano Mera, military leader of the CNT (Anarchist Labor Union of Syndicates) allied himself with the Junta, and one of the bloodiest battles of the war followed, with the Communists on one side and the Republicans and the CNT opposing the Communists. It is reported that Duran, on this occasion, deserted his assigned post, and lead his forces against the Republicans and the CNT in Madrid, Duran's forces being defeated in this action.

According to his own statement, Duran returned to Madrid after June, 1938, this directly contradicting the above-mentioned report that he joined the Communists infighting the Republican forces in Madrid. Regarding the alleged difficulty between certain Republican officers and the communists with respect to the surrender of Madrid, Duran has stated that he heard of a difference of opinion on this point, but declared that he knows of no actual violence which took place between the two factions. Duran has maintained that since he did not return to Madrid after June, 1938, he is not in a position to know what actually occurred there between the Communists and Republicans at the close of the war.

Duran has stated that prior to the surrender of Madrid, he had contacted Stewart Warner, American Consul and Colonel Fuqua, American Military Attache, as well as Mr. Ballantyne, the British Vice Consul, all of whom had been given information by Duran. After the surrender of Madrid, Duran unsuccessfully sought asylum in the American Embassy. However, through the Assistance of the British Vice-Consul Ballantyne, Duran was placed aboard a British destroyer at the port of Valencia, and was later transferred to the British hospital ship "Maine," which took Duran to Marseilles, France. From Marseilles, Duran made his way through Dieppe to London, where he was received by a British Relief organization for Spanish refugees. Duran has said that he did not enter the United States until 1940.

INDICATIONS OF POLITICAL SYMPATHIES AND ACTIVITIES OF GUSTAVO DURAN

Reports Received in the United States

Luis Bunuel, a Director of the Museum of Modern Art of New York City, has stated he has known Duran as a close personal friend since 1920, and lived with Duran in Spain. Bunuel advised that Duran's father committed suicide during the Civil war in Spain and that Duran and a brother have been at odds inasmuch as the brother was on the side of Franco and a confirmed Fascist, whereas Duran adhered to the Spanish constitutional Government and enlisted in the Loyalist Army on July 17, 1936 on the same date on which Bunuel enlisted. Bunuel stated that Duran is a very anti-Franco and anti- Fascist in his feelings.

A confidential informant stated that when the Spanish Civil War began Duran was a member of the Youth Socialist League, at which time that organization was affiliated with the Social Party of Spain under the second International. The informant stated that in December, 1936, the Youth Socialist League affiliated with the Communist Party of Spain, at which time Duran became a Communist and was an important figure in the Communist Party during the war. [This informant stated that Duran claims close personal friendship with Mrs. Roosevelt, wife of the President.]

Another confidential informant advised in July, 1942, that the Spanish Republican movement in Washington, D.C. had been reinforced by the moral support of Gustavo Duran, who at the time was said to be engaged in no activity. This source stated that the background of Duran is well known to the Spanish colony in Washington, and that ten percent of the Spanish Republicans are reported to be Communists.

A confidential informant advised Duran and his wife have entertained in their home in this country Mrs. Esmond Romilly, nee Jessica Mitford. It was reported that Jessica Mitford is a sister of Unity Mitford, who was reputed to be an intimate of Hitler prior to the war, and who is said to be presently interned in England with her husband, Sir Oswald Mosley.

Gustavo Duran has received correspondence from Mrs. William E. Beitz, subject of an investigation in Washington, D.C. looking toward denaturalizing (precedings). Mrs. Beitz is reported to be a naturalized United States citizen of German origin, who possesses pro-German sympathies, and was intimate with officials of the German Embassy in Washington, D.C. On December 5, 1942, Mrs. Beitz, using the address "Room 7705, Office of Coordinator of Inter-American Affairs, Washington, D.C." directed a letter to Duran at the American Embassy in Havana, Cuba. Mrs. Beitz stating that she had ascertained that "the FBI report on Gomez-Carrillo had been turned over, finally, to the personnel office." Bureau files reflect that a Aria Inez Gomez-Carilllo is an Argentine pianist who was hired by the United States Government at the suggestion of Mrs. Roosevelt, and who named Gustavo Duran as a reference.

(One sub-section heading redacted here and the next approximately three lines redacted.)

(One entire page redacted here.)

(Two-thirds of the next page redacted here.)

Gustavo Duran has made statements concerning the Communist Party in Spain and the part they played in the Spanish Civil war. Theses statements were made to a representative of the Bureau attached to the American Embassy in Havana, and in the course of his remarks, concerning the Communists, Duran constantly referred to them as "they" and never gave any indication that he personally was a member of the Communist Party. As noted above, Duran stated that he was not in Madrid after 1938, and declared that he was in no position to know whether the Communists fought against the Republicans and the CNT in Madrid.

INFORMATION CONCERNING ASSOCIATES AND SPONSORS OF GUSTAVO DURAN

Bonte Romilly Crompton

As previously mentioned, Gustavo Duran married Bonte Romilly Crompton in England on December 4, 1939. Duran's wife is the daughter of Mr. and Mrs. David Henry Crompton of Rye, New York and Wilton, New Hampshire. David Henry Crompton entered the United States in 1909 and became Vice President of the Booth shipping Company. Another daughter married Michael Straight of New York and England, who is presently reported to be employed by the United States Government and said to be a Socialist.

It is to be noted that the name "Bonte Crompton, Wilton, New Hampshire" was found among the papers of subject Leon W. Davis, of Detroit, Michigan, at the time of his apprehension by Bureau agents in the Detroit Spanish Enlistment Case on February 6, 1940. Upon interview, Davis stated that Bonte Crompton was a tourist whom he met during his travels in France.

George Kenneth Holland

When applying for employment by the United States Government, Gustavo Duran named Kenneth Holland of the Office of Coordinator of Inter-American affairs as a reference. It developed that this reference had known Gustavo Duran for approximately one year, and stated that he knew no derogatory information concerning Duran. It is to be noted that George Kenneth Holland, a Director of the Office of Coordinator of Inter-American Affairs, Office of Emergency Management, was investigated by the Bureau in a Hatch Act Case based on information that Holland was listed in the indices of the Communist Front organizations "American Peace Mobilization" and the "Washington Committee for Democratic Action." No administrative action was taken by the Office for Emergency Management upon receipt of the Bureau's report in the matter.

Luis Bunuel

This individual, a Director of the Museum of Modern Art of New York City, has been previously mentioned as a close personal friend of Gustavo Duran since 1920. Luis Bunuel was also named as a reference by Duran in seeking a United States Government position, and Bunuel gave a favorable recommendation. The Bureau files reflect that Luis Bunuel, a native of Spain, originally entered the United States on September 25, 1938, under a Diplomatic Visa, admittedly representing the Government of Spain for the purpose of engaging in propaganda work for the Spanish Republican Government. It is reported that Bunuel left Spain with the assistance of two Spaniards who are described as definitely linked with the Community Party, one of whom is said to be an International Agent of the Party. Bunuel was originally denied a United States Immigration Visa in view of his connections with the Spanish Republican Government and the suggestion that Bunuel was either a Communist or a fellow traveler. However, a Vice Board of Appeals finally granted an Immigration Visa to Bunuel upon his assertion that he was not a member of the Communist Party. As previously mentioned, Bunuel enlisted in the Spanish Loyalist Army with Gustavo Duran on July 17, 1936.

Charles Seeger

This individual was also named by Gustavo Duran as a reference in applying for a position with the United States Government, and a favorable recommendation was given for Duran by Charles Seeger. The Bureau files reveal that the name of Charles Seeger appeared on the active indices of the Communist Front organization "American Peace Mobilization," no investigation being conducted inasmuch as Seeger was removed from the Government pay roll, and became employed by the Pan American Union.

Ernest Hemingway

The activities of Ernest Hemingway in connection with Anti-Fascist and Communist Front organizations in the United States are well known. In August, 1942, Hemingway volunteered his services to the American Ambassador in Havana, offering to assist in intelligence work in Cuba. The Ambassador asked the opinion of the Bureau Legal Attache in the matter, and was advised that Hemingway signed a petition denouncing the FBI in regard to the Detroit Spanish Enlistment Case in 1940, and had more recently referred to the FBI as "the American Gestapo." Nevertheless, the Ambassador engaged the services of Hemingway, who set up an intelligence organization consisting of paid informants, the entire activity being under the personal direction of the

American Ambassador. In August, 1942, Hemingway suggested that Gustavo Duran be transferred from his Government position in the United States to assist Hemingway in his intelligence activities in Cuba. The arrangement was to be a temporary one for a period of thirty days, during which time Duran was to take charge of Hemingway's intelligence organization while Hemingway was absent on a mission for the Naval Attache in connection with anti-submarine activities. Hemingway assured the Ambassador that Duran is a military and intelligence genius, who "is "pure Republican and not a Communist," who would be able to obtain complete information concerning the Spanish Falange in Cuba.

Although the American Ambassador was advised by the Bureau Legal Attache that Gustavo Duran was at that time actually an employee of the Office of Coordinator of Inter-American Affairs, the Ambassador took the position that if Duran was transferred to the Embassy, he would be working directly under the Ambassador. Duran arrived in Cuba in November, 1942, and began working with Hemingway, "The "intelligence coverage" of Hemingway consisted of vague and unfounded reports of a sensational character. Duran's work in Cuba has not been of the same sensational character as Hemingway's, but the reports which have been submitted through Duran are, nonetheless, unspecific and unverified. Duran attempted to accomplish a coverage of public opinion in Cuba, which he submitted in reports untitled "The Voice of the Street," These reports have contained statements made by persons in cafes, bars, and poolrooms, and, thus, do not represent a fair cross section of general public opinion in Cuba. In February, 1943, Ernest Hemingway and Gustavo Duran submitted information to the American Ambassador charging that Special Agent H.E. Knoblaugh, assigned to the Embassy as Assistant Legal Attache, was a participant of the Franco Movement in Spain, and had acted as a paid Franco propagandist. These charges were based on the fact that Special Agent Knoblaugh had written a book "Correspondent in Spain" upon his return from Madrid as an Associated Press correspondent in 1938. Although Hemingway had been ostensibly friendly with Special Agent Knoblaugh in Spain, Hemingway had no discussion with Special Agent Knoblaugh concerning the book, and took the charges directly to the Ambassador. The Ambassador later admitted to the Bureau Legal Attache that he had read only a few pages of the book, and after requesting the Legal Attache to have Special Agent Knoblaugh assigned to some other post, the Ambassador dismissed the subject as having no further importance. Hemingway and Duran are known to have a low esteem of the work of the FBI, which they consider to be "methodical and unimaginative."

PRESENT STATUS OF GUSTAVO DURAN IN THE AMERICAN EMBASSY, HAVANA, CUBA

The services of Ernest Hemingway in intelligence matters were ostensibly discontinued by the American Ambassador on April 1, 1942. The Embassy is still receiving a few reports relating to cases previously investigated by Hemingway's organization and directed to Gustavo Duran. It is also known that Hemingway is continuing a project on behalf of the Naval attache in Havana, which consists of an investigation of enemy submarine and clandestine radio activity off the coast of Cuba.

While the investigation of subversive activity suspects as such had been ostensibly discontinued by Hemingway, the American Ambassador has requested that Gustavo Duran continue to submit reports on public opinion in Cuba as was previously undertaken in the "Voice of the Street" reports. The Ambassador feels that these reports give an "inside picture" of public opinion in Cuba, and are received with great interest by the State Department. Duran is now employed by the Embassy in Havana on a permanent basis as a member of the Auxiliary Foreign Service, and Duran employees the services of a few informants at a cost of around $200 a month. Duran also analyzes political comments and articles appearing in the Cuban newspapers and assists the Ambassador in preparing speeches to be given in the Spanish language.

The Bureau Legal Attache has recently reported that Gustavo Duran is evidencing no spirit of hostility toward FBI representatives in Cuba, and Duran has been cordial and helpful. The Bureau Legal Attache is aware of no instance in which Duran has taken an undue interest in FBI operations in Cuba, which might indicate an ulterior purpose on the part of Duran. However, all of the FBI reports pass through a section of the Embassy where Duran is employed, giving him the opportunity to be aware of all FBI activities in Cuba as reported to the Embassy.

SUMMARY

(Two complete paragraphs redacted here, each about six-to eight lines long.)

A reliable source in the United States has reported that Gustavo Duran was a member of the Youth Socialist League at the beginning of the Spanish Civil War, and became a member of the Communist Party of Spain when the Youth Socialist League affiliated with the Party in December, 1936.

As has been previously mentioned, three sponsors of Gustavo Duran in the United States have been reported to be connected in some degree with Communist Party of Communist Front activities.

(One third of the first line of this paragraph is redacted) report that Gustavo Duran took his forces to Madrid during the closing days of the Spanish Civil War and fought along-side the Communist forces in opposing the surrender of the city to Franco. According to Duran's one statement, he never returned to Madrid after June, 1938. It is noted that Duran's statement that he was unaware of any violence between the Communists and Republicans in Madrid appears to be inconsistent with rather widespread information circulated at the time concerning the disorder in Madrid based on refusal of the Communists to join in a surrender of Madrid to Franco.

It has been suggested that the following sources of information might be contacted for evidence of membership in the Communist Party on the part of Gustavo Duran:

(Two separate paragraphs redacted here; each about six lines long.)

A check of the records of the State Department and the War Department might reveal information concerning Duran as reported by the American Embassy in Madrid.

RECOMMENDATIONS

(Two separate paragraphs redacted here; the first paragraph about six lines long, the second six-to-eight lines long.)

It is further suggested that a blind memorandum be prepared setting out all information previously mentioned concerning the activities of Gustavo Duran, and that this blind memorandum be furnished to Mr. Berle and the State department with the confidential request that the Bureau be furnished all information contained in their files concerning the activities of Gustavo Duran in Spain and elsewhere in Europe. (This last part of the paragraph is redacted, approximately four and one-half lines.)

It is further pointed out that in discussing this entire matter with Mr. Berle, it should be kept in mind that Gustavo Duran is reported to be a close friend of Ernest Hemingway and American Ambassador Spruille Braden in Cuba.

Respectfully,

D.M. Ladd

A script note appears below; probably the same signer who added a note to the previous August 21, 1943 memorandum by C.H. Carson:

I agree

On September 20, 1943, D.M. Ladd sends J. Edgar Hoover an up-date memorandum about Hemingway.

Federal Bureau of Investigation
United States Department of Justice
Washington, D.C.

September 20, 1943

MEMORANDUM FOR THE DIRECTOR

RE: ERNEST HEMINGWAY

<u>Background</u>

You will recall that for a time Ernest Hemingway was engaged in intelligence activities at the request of and under the direct supervision of the American Ambassador in Havana, Cuba. As of April 1, 1943, however, the Ambassador dispensed with the intelligence services of Hemingway, and it was indicated that Hemingway's organization of confidential informants in Cuba would no longer render reports on intelligence matters. The Bureau Legal Attache in Havana has ascertained that Hemingway has since April 1, 1943, continued operations in Cuba on behalf of the United States Naval Attache; that is, operations consisting of cruising the waters off the coast of Cuba in a small boat for the purpose of ascertaining the extent of enemy submarine activities.

Details

(One complete paragraph redacted here, approximately 10 lines.)

During the week of September 12, 1943, the New York columnist Leonard Lyons stated in his column that Ernest Hemingway had departed from Cuba, without further elaboration.

The Bureau Legal Attache in Havana advised that Hemingway departed from Cuba on September 19, 1943 on another submarine patrol trip in the Caribbean area, accompanied by Winston Guest, and expected to be gone for approximately two months, after which Hemingway stated he would proceed to New York for a vacation of approximately six weeks. Prior to his departure on this most recent patrol trip, Hemingway advised a SIS Representative that he is doing no writing at the present time whatsoever but is considering three plots for use in writing books during the post-war period. Hemingway has made no further reference to the proposed book that he was previously reported to be writing concerning his intelligence experiences in Cuba.

Martha Gellhorn Hemingway, wife of Ernest, is presently in New York arranging for publication of a book which she has reportedly written concerning conditions on the Island of Martinique, based in part upon intelligence which Martha Gellhorn obtained from the State Department through the assistance of a United States official in Havana.

There has been reported no change in the situation existing between Hemingway and the American Embassy in Havana, and Hemingway apparently enjoys the full confidence of Ambassador Spruille Braden and is continuing his activities on behalf of the United States Naval Attache. Despite the ostensible discontinuance of Hemingway's intelligence activities for the Ambassador on April 1, 1943, The Bureau Legal Attache has ascertained that Hemingway has a quantity of gasoline charged to him from the private stock of the Ambassador for the month of April, 1943, indicating an actual continuance of an arrangement which had been previously in effect for the benefit of Hemingway's intelligence organization to April 1, 1943. (The rest of this paragraph is redacted, approximately six-seven lines.)

ACTION

(One complete paragraph redacted here, approximately ten to twelve lines.)

Respectfully,

D.M. Ladd

On September 21, 1943, a three-page memorandum is sent to J. Edgar Hoover, from CONE. INFT. S.I.S. #396 in Havana. Material underlined appears to have been underlined in pencil.

OFFICE OF THE LEGAL ATTACHE

EMBASSY OF THE
UNITED STATES OF AMERICA
HAVANA, CUBA

September 21, 1943

Director,
Federal Bureau of Investigation
Washington, D.C.

Re: Ernest Hemingway
Cuba Latin American Matters

Dear Sir;

On September 13, 1945, SIS <u>#213 accepted an invitation to have lunch with Subject</u> at his finca located in San Francisco 15 kilometers from Havana. There was <u>no other person present.</u> <u>Hemingway was quite talkative but kept away from controversial subjects</u>. He revealed that MARTHA GELLHORN HEMINGWAY, <u>his present wife, left for the United States</u> the first week in September, and <u>planned to talk with her publishers about the book which she has been writing for the past few months</u>. Hemingway had previously informed the writer that he had proofread the work of his wife, and was convinced that she had something worth while. He further revealed that after conferring with her publishers, it was her intention to join the Allied Forces invading Europe as a correspondent for Colliers. She is expected to be gone for five or six months.

<u>Hemingway stated that he is tired of being on land with nothing to do and is anxious to return to his confidential work</u> (which, we are confidentially advised is patrol duty in the Caribbean waters on behalf of the U.S. Navy). On September 13, 1943, he stated that he <u>expected to leave on or before the 20th</u> but in conversation with him on September 20, he told the

writer that he would not be able to leave before September 22 or 23 due to delay in repairs to his boat. As in the past, he is to be accompanied by WINSTON GUEST and a small crew. He explained that the usual procedure is to patrol for twelve hours, ostensibly fishing, and tie up at whatever dock is convenient every night. This particular trip is expected to last approximately two months. At the <u>expiration of this trip, Hemingway plans to spend from six to eight weeks in New York City and Long Island</u> making the rounds of the night spots and duck shooting on Long Island, as he expressed it.

<u>Concerning the picture "For Whom the Bell Tolls," Hemingway stated that he has no desire to see it because he does not believe it is a true portrayal of his work</u>. He further declared that Sam Wood, the director, did not like the book, and, therefore, was unable to approach his task with a sympathetic viewpoint. Furthermore, Gary Cooper is past his prime and he does not consider his choice was leading man a happy one.

Under date of July 12,1943, the file contains the following memorandum of information obtained by the Legal Attache in conversation with Robert R. Joyce, former Second Secretary of the American Embassy:

"The picture based on Hemingway's book, 'For Whom the Bell Tolls,' will be presented for the first time at the Paramount Theater in New York City on July 14, 1943. Hemingway was invited to the premiere but refused; his wife, Martha Gellhorn Hemingway, was later invited and likewise declined. Their declination is a result of their dissatisfaction with the manner in which the film company adapted the book for screen presentation. Hemingway received a letter from Gary Cooper, who plays the principal role, stating the teeth had been pulled from the story and the result was a meaningless war romance cast against the Spanish countryside.

"Hemingway has refused to see the advance shots of the picture, though requested to come to Hollywood or New York at the film company's expense, feeling that the film executives intend to salve him into a state of submission to the mutilation of his story. He <u>considers himself free to attack the picture when it appears because he did not O.K. the revision. He still threatens to expose the 'Fascist influences' namely the Vatican and certain State Department officials sympathetic to Franco, who were responsible for the 'castration' of his book</u>."

The conversation turned to writing. He stated that at the present time, he was only catching up on some old correspondence. He said that he is not writing any books at the present time, but has three plots in mind which he thinks will form the basis for good stories. These concern his experiences in the past year. However, he does not intend to use these plots until the war is over. <u>In connection with this, Hemingway told SIS #396 on August 24, 1943 that he would never write anything about his intelligence work on behalf of the Ambassador</u>. If he wrote anything as a result of his present experiences, he would limit it to a fictional story based on anti-submarine work. At the time of his conversation with SIS #396, he stated that he had prepared nothing.

Ina discussion of columnists, Hemingway stated that DREW PEARSON is known to him only slightly. However, he has always believed that in his search for sensational stories, he frequently makes statements that are only half truths. As an example of his tendency, he referred to an article that Pearson had written in his column, "The Daily Washington Merry-Go-Round," <u>in which Pearson stated that individuals who had fought in the Abraham Lincoln Brigade in the Spanish Civil War were discriminated against by U.S. Army authorities when they sought admission to Officers' Training School. Although Hemingway</u>

thinks that members of the Abraham Lincoln Brigade have been the subjects of discrimination, he stated that Pearson was unfortunate in his choice of examples. According to Hemingway, each individual that Pearson claimed was refused admission to Officers' Training School was an out and out Communist' having attended a Communist Indoctrination School located in the Catskill Mountains in New York State- In these instances, Hemingway affirmed that the Army was justified in the action which was taken.

Regarding his work, Hemingway stated that he never intended to find himself in any such line of activity. His explanation for organizing an intelligence service which was in operation until April 1, 1943, was that he did so when specifically requested to do so by the Ambassador, who believed that he was eminently qualified to aid the Embassy in gathering information about the Spanish Falange because of his long association with Spaniards.

Very truly yours,

[CONF. INFT. S.I.S. #396]

Legal Attache

J. Edgar Hoover sent a memorandum to an S.I.S. agent in Havana. (The original radiogram to the FBI in Washington apparently no longer exists.) In the third paragraph, he writes: "It is suggested that this letter should be destroyed when it has served your purpose."

October 14, 1943

[S.I.S. #396]

Re: Ernest Hemingway
Latin American Matters

Dear Sir;

Reference is made to your radiogram dated September 18, 1943, concerning a book which had previously reported to be under consideration by Ernest Hemingway, the subject matter to be based on his intelligence experiences in Cuba.

(One full paragraph redacted here, approximately six and one half lines.)

It is further requested that the Bureau be kept advised as to the whereabouts of Ernest Hemingway and as to the date of his departure from Cuba to the United States.

It is suggested that this letter should be destroyed when it has served your purposes.

Very truly yours,

John Edgar Hoover

Director

There begins to be long gaps in the Hemingway FBI records beginning at this period, as Hemingway left Cuba for the European theater of World War Two. The next entry is a short memorandum to J. Edgar Hoover, dated May 22, 1944, apparently from the New York City Bureau of the FBI. Underlined material appears to have been underlined in pencil. Ernest is a "great admirer of you and the Bureau" seems to be something of a misstatement.

New York, 7, N.Y.

May 22, 1944

Mr. HOOVER–

RE: ERNEST HEMINGWAY

<u>Ernest is a great admirer of you and the Bureau</u>. In a conversation with an agent of this Office, he stated that he had <u>met several of the Bureau representatives while in Havana, Cuba, and he thought that they were of an unusually high type and, further, that their work was most effective</u> there. He stated that he had been very friendly with General Benitz, who was a ranking political power in Cuba, and he thought it was most amazing the General should hold his present position inasmuch as some years ago Benitz had acted in several Hollywood pictures in which he played "Latin lover" roles.

E.E. CONROY

A two-age memorandum is prepared about Hemingway, by the FBI in Washington. Under the end of this memorandum is a notation: Blind Memorandum for Transmittal to the Office of the Secretary of Defense. ("Blind" may mean: without credit to the FBI — it also appears on blank paper, without an FBI letterhead.)

August 30, 1949

MEMORANDUM

Re: ERNEST HEMINGWAY

Abraham Lincoln Brigade

In May, 1938, Ernest Hemingway was reported to be a contributor to the publication "Among Friends," a quarterly magazine put out by the Friends of the Abraham Lincoln Brigade. The publication was described as being devoted to the Loyalists' cause in Spain and more particularly to the Abraham Lincoln Brigade.

The "Daily Worker" of February 3, 1939, announced that Ernest Hemingway would speak on February 22, 1939, at a memorial meeting to be held in honor of the men who dies fighting for the Abraham Lincoln Brigade. The "Daily Worker"' is an East Coast daily Communist newspaper.

In June, 1939, Hemingway's name was listed on the letterhead of the Abraham Lincoln Brigade as one of its sponsors.

The Attorney General has cited the Abraham Lincoln Brigade as being within the purview of Executive Order 9835.

American Committee for the Protection of Foreign Born

In January, 1940, Ernest Hemingway addressed letters over his personal signature endorsing the work of the American Committee for the Protection of Foreign Born and soliciting the assistance of various persons. He requested that any contribution in the form of checks be made payable to him.

A circular soliciting sponsors for the American Committee for the Protection of Foreign Born was distributed at the Fourth Annual Conference of that organization held in Washington, D.C. on March 2 and 3, 1940. The circular was signed jointed by Ernest Hemingway and Dr. William Allen Neilson as Co-Chairmen for the Committee of Sponsors.

Ernest Hemingway was listed as a sponsor of the American Committee for the Protection of Foreign Born as of August, 1940. Conference of the American Committee for the Protection of Foreign Born which was scheduled to be held in Atlantic City on March 29 and 30, 1941.

The American Committee for the Protection of Foreign Born was declared by the attorney general to be within the purview of Executive Order 9835.

American Rescue Ship Mission

The January 19, 1941 issue of the "Daily Worker" published an article bearing the headline "Hemingway Reaffirms Backing of Rescue Ship Mission." The article quoted a cable received from Hemingway in Havana in which he expressed the sincere hope that a ship would be obtained "as soon as it is humanly possible to do so."

The American Rescue Ship Mission has been declared by the Attorney General to be within the purview of Executive Order 9835.

League of American Writers

On February 21, 1941 Ernest Hemingway was reported as being a Vice- President and a member of the Board of Directors of the League of American Writers, Incorporated.

The League of American Writers has been cited by the Attorney General as being within the purview of Executive Order 9835.

Miscellaneous

A reliable informant has reported that during the period 1942–1943, Ernest Hemingway repeatedly asserted that he was anti-Communist and that he was as much opposed to the Communist influence in the Spanish war as he was to the Fascist.

A reliable informant has reported that in September, 1943, Ernest Hemingway was discussing certain newspaper articles which attacked the United States Army for refusing to admit to the Officers' Training School individuals who had fought in the Abraham Lincoln Brigade in the Spanish Civil War. According to the informant, Hemingway took exception and stated that he United States Army was perfectly justified in the action which was taken inasmuch as each individual who had been refused admission to the Officers' Training School was an out-and-out Communist.

The FBI prepares another blind memorandum for the Office of Secretary of Defense. The date on this memorandum is obscured by stamps which read:

ALL INFORMATION CONTAINED
HEREIN IS UNCLASSIFIED
EXCEPT WHERE SHOWN

It cannot be determined whether this memorandum pre-dates or follows the previous blind memorandum, but this memorandum probably follows the earlier document.

SUBJECT: REQUEST FROM THE OFFICE OF THE
         SECRETARY OF DEFENSE FOR NAME CHECK
         ON ERNEST HEMINGWAY

Attached hereto is a blind memorandum prepared in response to a request from the Office of the Secretary of Defense for a check of FBI files, to include a summary of any information which "would affect clearance for access to highly classified material."

In addition to the information set out in the blind memorandum it is noted that Bureau files show that Ernest Hemingway operated an intelligence organization for the American Ambassador in Havana, Cuba from August 1942 to April 1943. During this period Hemingway was in frequent contact with the Office of the Legal Attache at Havana, Cuba.

The Legal Attache reported in June 1943 that in personal relations Hemingway maintained a surface show of friendship and interest with representatives of the FBI. Through statements he made to reliable contacts of the Legal Attache, however, it as known that Hemingway and his assistant Gustavo Duran, had a low esteem for the work of the FBI which they considered to be methodical, unimaginative, and performed by persons of comparative youth without experience in foreign countries and knowledge of international intrigue and politics. Both Hemingway and Duran, it was also known, had personal hostility to the FBI on an ideological basis, especially Hemingway; that he considered the FBI anti-Liberal, pro-Fascist, and dangerous of developing into an American Gestapo.

It is noted that Ernest Hemingway was a principal signer of the denunciation of the FBI in the Detroit Communist-Spanish Enlistment Case in 1940. In addition the Legal Attache advised that on meeting Hemingway some weeks previously the latter had referred to the FBI as "The American Gestapo." At the request of the Legal Attache Hemingway was sounded out by a representative of the Embassy at Havana concerning these remarks. The Embassy representative later return with the advise that Hemingway stated he had paid no particular attention to the petition he had signed in 1940 denouncing the FBI and could now hardly remember what it said; Hemingway told the Embassy representative that people were always shoving petitions under his nose and like many famous people he was inclined to sign them on a request of a friend without full information as to their contents. Hemingway also reportedly dismissed the reference to the FBI as "The American Gestapo" as a mere jest.

In addition to the organizations mentioned in the attached blind memorandum, it is noted that Bureau files reflect Hemingway's past affiliation with such organizations as the Medical Bureau to Aid Spanish Democracy, American Relief Ship Mission for Spain, and the American Writers' Congress. None of these organizations are on the Attorney General's list and the Bureau has not established Hemingway's membership in these organizations by investigation.

ACTION:

It is recommended that the information developed concerning Hemingway during his service to the American Ambassador in Havana, Cuba, not be made available to the Office of the Secretary of Defense since this information is largely of an administrative nature and does not appear to be such as would affect clearance for access to highly classified material. It is also recommended that the information associating Hemingway with the organizations mentioned above not be made available to the requesting agency since these organizations are not on the Attorney General's list.

If the attached blind memorandum meets with your approval, it is recommended that it be returned to Room 6733 for transmittal to the Office of the Secretary of Defense.

Finally the world discovered, in small part, Hemingway's activities in Cuba. FBI files indicate this was published in The Washington Post. A date stamp shows it was entered into the FBI files Jan. 12, 1954.

Hemingway Helped
Spy, Saboteur Hunt

NEW YORK, Dec. 22 — Novelist Ernest Hemingway ran an underground "crime shop" in Cuba during World War II to help American agents track down saboteurs and spies aiding the enemy sinking allied shipping in the Caribbean Sea, it was disclosed today.

Spruille Braden, former Assistant Secretary of State, said that when he was Ambassador to Cuba in 1942, he arranged with Hemingway for the establishment of this counterspy apparatus.

The apparatus was headed, Braden said, by Gustavo Duran, an international mystery man and Hemingway's "inspiration" for the hero of "For Whom the Bell Tools."

The next two FBI documents are, perhaps, the most bizarre entries in the Hemingway file.

The first FBI Bureau file on this matter, dated August 26, 1954, begins on one page; the final two paragraphs of six on the first page are redacts, the entire next two pages are completely redacted, as well as three paragraphs on the fourth page, amounting to about two-thirds of the fourth, or final, page.

The material not redacted on page one explained that Edward "Ted" Scott, a British subject, living in Havana and writing for the English language Havana Post, in a column titled "Interesting If True" indicated that Hemingway's fourth wife Mary said that lion steaks were very delectable. Scott took issue with this statement; whereupon Mary Hemingway called him a "stupid British colonial." Scott then challenged Hemingway himself to a duel. A duel! In Havana in 1954! The second file, dated September 1, 1954, states that Hemingway declined, indicating that he was in ill health, had a lot of writing to do and "a court of honor would not consider this cowardice on his part."

Scott advised that although he was not satisfied with Hemingway's answer he did not know what else he could do about it.

The FBI prepares another blind memorandum about Hemingway, presumably to be sent to any federal government agency that requested information about him.

> July 20, 1955
> ERNEST HEMINGWAY
> Born: July 21, 1899
> Oak Park, Illinois

No investigation pertinent to your inquiry has been conducted by the FBI concerning the captioned individual. However, the files of this Bureau reflect the following information which may relate to the subject of your name check request.

Abraham Lincoln Brigade

The "New York Times" of May 8, 1938, reported that Ernest Hemingway was a contributor to the publication "Among Friends," a quarterly magazine put out by the Friends of the Abraham Lincoln Brigade. The publication was described as being devoted to the Loyalists' cause in Spain and more particularly to the Abraham Lincoln Brigade.

The "Daily Worker" of February 3, 1939, announced that Ernest Hemingway would speak on February 22, 1939, at a memorial meeting to be held in honor of the men who died fighting in the Abraham Lincoln Brigade. The "Daily Worker" is an east coast daily Communist newspaper.

A confidential informant who has furnished reliable information in the past made available a letter dated June 21, 1936, bearing the letterhead of the Friends of the Abraham Lincoln Brigade on which the name Ernest Hemingway appeared as a sponsor.

The Attorney General has cited the Abraham Lincoln Brigade as being within the purview of Executive Order 10450.

American Committee for Protection of Foreign Born

Another government agency advised in October, 1941, that the American Committee for Protection of Foreign Born held its Fourth Annual Conference in Washington, D.C., on March 2 and 3, 1940 at which circulars were disseminated. These circulators were signed jointly by an other individual and Ernest Hemingway as co-chairman for the Committee of Sponsors.

The American Committee for Protection of Foreign Born was declared by the Attorney General to be within the purview of Executive Order 10450.

American Rescue Ship Mission

The January 16, 1941 issue of the "Daily Worker" published an article bearing the headline "Hemingway Reaffirms Backing of Rescue Ship Mission." The article quoted a cable received from Hemingway in Havana in which he expressed the sincere hope that a ship would be obtained "as soon as it's humanly possible to do so."

The American Rescue Ship Mission has been declared by the Attorney General to be within the purview of Executive Order 10450.

League of American Writers

Volume 401-78 of the Membership Corporation, State of New York, from July 5, 1939, to August 19, 1939, contains the Certificate of Incorporation of the League of American Writers, Inc. Ernest Hemingway, Box 406, Key West, Florida was listed as a member of the Board of Directors.

The League of American Writers has been cited by the Attorney General as being within the purview of Executive Order 10450.

Miscellaneous

A confidential informant who has previously furnished reliable information reported that in September, 1943, Ernest Hemingway was discussing certain newspaper articles which attacked the United States Army for refusing to admit to the Officers' Training School individuals who had fought in the Abraham Lincoln Brigade in the Spanish Civil War. According to the informant, Hemingway took exception and stated that the United States Army was perfectly justified in the action which was taken inasmuch as each individual who had been refused admission to the Officers' Training School was an out-and-out Communist.

The foregoing information is furnished to you as the result of a request for an FBI file check and it not to be construed as a clearance or a nonclearance of the individual involved. This information is furnished for your use and should not be disseminated outside of your agency.

The next entry in the Hemingway file is an article clipped from the Washington D.C. Star, of approximately August 11, 1958, reporting an unsuccessful attempt by Hemingway to prevent Esquire magazine from reprinting some of his much earlier articles about the Spanish Civil War. We have reprinted the first paragraph (only) from the Star article, here.

Hemingway's Suit

A lot of people in the writing game will understand why Ernest Hemingway has filed suit to prevent Esquire magazine from republishing some of his old stories about the Spanish Civil War. Back in those days, two decades ago, he was a strong supporter of the Loyalists against Generalissimo Franco, and the stories in question reflected his sentiments of that period. But now, even though he still adheres to that sentiment, he apparently wishes he had written them in a different way. Anyhow, he doesn't want to see them in print again in their original form, which makes him not unlike numerous lesser writers who are embarrassed when confronted with certain of their past works that look slightly unpolished or naive in retrospect.

The next file is a Foreign Service dispatch from the American Embassy, in Havana to the Department of State, Washington, regarding Hemingway's thoughts about the Cuban revolution.

FOREIGN SERVICE DISPATCH

From American Embassy, HAVANA   November 6, 1959

To THE DEPARTMENT OF STATE, WASHINGTON

SUBJECT: Ernest HEMINGWAY Gives Views on Cuban Situation

<u>BEGIN UNCLASSIFIED</u>

For many years past, perhaps the most famous American resident in Cuba has been Ernest Hemingway, who has a home in San Francisco de Paula, near Havana, where he spends a large part of his time. Hemingway generally lives a retired life there, together with his wife and frequent visitors.

Hemingway returned from a long visit to Spain on November 3, 1959. He was interviewed at the airport by Prensa Latina, and contrary to his usual custom, made several statements on the local situation and his reaction. Among other things, he said, as quoted by Prensa Latina:

1) His opinion of the Revolutionary Government was unchanged since January—he supported it and all its acts completely, and thought it was the best thing that has ever happened in Cuba.

2) He had not believed any of the information published abroad against Cuba. He sympathized with the Cuban government, and all our difficulties.

3) Hemingway emphasized the <u>our</u>, and was asked about it. He said that he hoped Cubans would regard him not as a <u>Yanqui</u> (his word) but another Cuban. With that, he kissed a Cuban flag which was nearby. He refused to repeat the gesture for photographers, saying that he "had kissed the flag with sincerity", implying that publicity would cheapen the act.

4) Hemingway said he knew nothing about any recent note from the American Government to the Cuban Government on relations between the two countries. He said that he had come from New York, where they "knew nothing about Cuba or the world. There all they talked about is Van Doren and the scandal of the TV quiz shows."

BEGIN OFFICIAL USE ONLY

Comment: Hemingway's remarks have been strongly played by Prensa Latina, and given wide publicity locally. It is unfortunate that because of his position and reputation should publicly take a position which displays either (1) strong criticism of his government and compatriots, or (2) a remarkable ignorance concerning developments in Cuba since the first of the year.

END OFFICIAL USE ONLY

For the Ambassador:
Daniel M. Braddock
Minister-Counselor

The next entry is the most dramatic in the FBI-Hemingway files. It was sent from the Minneapolis FBI Bureau to the Director's office in Washington. SAC is the abbreviation for Special Agent in Charge, a Bureau Chief of a FBI office.

A doctor at the Mayo Clinic or a Mayo Clinic administrator may have called the FBI Bureau in Minneapolis to obtain authorization to inform Hemingway there was no FBI objection about Hemingway's registration under an assumed name. Presumably the FBI learned Hemingway's medical condition from this telephone call or contact (paragraph two).

Date 1/13/61

TO: DIRECTOR, FBI   PERSONAL ATTENTION
FROM: SAC, MINNEAPOLIS
RE: ERNEST HEMINGWAY
    INFORMATION CONCERNING

ERNEST HEMINGWAY, the author, has been a patient at Mayo Clinic, Rochester, Minnesota, and is presently at St. Mary's Hospital in that city. He has been at the Clinic for several weeks and is described as a problem. He is seriously ill, both physically and mentally, and at one time the doctors were considering giving him electro-shock therapy treatments.

(One half line redacted here) Mayo Clinic, advised to eliminate publicity and contacts by newsmen, the Clinic had suggested Mr. HEMINGWAY register under the alias GEORGE SEVIER, (about three words redacted here) stated that Mr. HEMINGWAY is now worried about his registering under an assumed name, and is concerned about an FBI investigation. (About two words redacted here) stated that inasmuch as this worry was interfering with the treatments of Mr. HEMINGWAY, he desired authorization to tell HEMINGWAY that the FBI was not concerned with his registering under an assumed name (about two or three words redacted here) was advised there was no objection.

Hemingway was treated at the Mayo Clinic for uncontrolled high blood pressure, liver disease, diabetes and depression. He did receive electro-shock treatments at the Mayo Clinic, which caused him to lose his memory and the ability to write.

Ernest Hemingway used a personal shotgun to commit suicide early July 2, 1961, in Ketchum, Idaho. He is buried there.

Thereafter the FBI files contain a clipping of a column "As Pegler Sees It," by Westbrook Pegler, date-stamped Jul 17 1961. Pegler, an acerbic columnist, won a Pulitzer Prize for investigative reporting in 1941, exposing corruption in Hollywood, but he was critical of every President from Hoover to John Kennedy. By the early 1960s, he was too extreme even for the then-popular John Birch Society.
The first paragraph of his column appears below.
Pegler is now forgotten; Hemingway remains a literary icon.

It has been my stubborn opinion that Ernest Hemingway was actually one of the worst writers in the English language during his time. It can be conceded that he invented a "style." But to me is was an ugly style, so barren of ordinary literary embellishment or amenity that it was confused and often incomprehensible.

The files continue with a relatively meaningless letter from writer Quentin Reynolds to J. Edgar Hoover, dated January 6, 1964, beginning "I'm sure that this is a tempest in a teapot." — with numerous redactions — and a short reply from Hoover to Reynolds.

In 1974, University of Florida librarians wrote to then FBI Director Clarence Kelley regarding obtaining FBI files for the library, specifically files on Elizabeth Bentley, Whittaker Chambers, Hemingway and John Dos Passos. Kelley sends a form letter of reply.

The files contain a clipping from the New York Times dated Sep 12 1974 regarding a film company which wanted to make a film for television in Cuba about Hemingway and his life there. (The film was apparently never made.)

The files contain about seven additional pages; none of them seem to have any specific reference to Hemingway.

And there they end. As T.S. Eliot wrote, in "The Hollow Men" (1925):

> *This is the way the world ends*
> *Not with a bang but a whimper*

What became of the principal figures cited in the FBI files?

Gustavo Duran went on to a career with the United Nations, serving in New York, Chile, the Congo and Greece from 1946 to 1969.

In the early 1950s, he was caught up in the Joe McCarthy-Red Scare scandals. He became, at least momentarily, the focus of McCarthy. An article "Weighted in the Balance," in Time, Oct. 22, 1951, states:

> A favorite McCarthy victim these days is Gustavo Duran. Joe flourishes as pictures of Duran taken during the Spanish Civil War in what he says is "the uniform of the S.I.M. — the counterpart of the Russian secret police." He then says that Duran's American citizenship was rushed through, that he was "promoted" by the State Department to the U.N. in 1946. "And what do you think he was doing there today? Unbelievable as it is, his ask was to screen displayed persons and decide which would make good, loyal Americans!"
>
> The true story of Duran is remarkable — but nothing like McCarthy's version. Duran was a Spanish composer of music who fought in the Spanish Republican Army,

rising to command of a corps. As the Spanish Loyalists split into Communist and anti-Communist factions, Duran, never a Red, was definitely and clearly anticommunist. When defeat came, he was smuggled out of Spain on a British warship, he married an American, became a citizen in four months more than the time required by law, worked for the U.S. Government in Cuba during World War II, tracking down Axis and Communist agents. For the past five years, Duran has been working for the U.N., where he has never had anything to do with screening refugees entering the U.S. The uniform in which McCarthy shows Duran is that of the Spanish army, not of any secret police. McCarthy knows all this — but his audiences do not.

Duran was the U.N. representative in Luluabourg and Stanleyville in 1961-1962 and political officer in charge of U.N. operations in the Congo 1962-1965. Then he moved to Greece. He had a series of heart attacks, beginning in 1961.

He wanted to go back to Spain but died in Athens in 1969.

Ambassador Spruille Braden held brief Ambassadorships in Columbia, 1939-1942 and then in Cuba, in 1942. He served as Assistant Secretary of State for Western Hemisphere Affairs under President Harry Truman, in 1944. He also was Ambassador in Argentina (1945), Guatemala (1953-1954) and Chile (1975-1976). Wikipedia states "His diplomatic activities in these countries often coincided with coups d'etates and other interventions in internal politics."

He published his memoirs Diplomats and Demagogues *in 1971.*

Braden died in 1978.

Winston Guest, called Wolf or Wolfe, who was British, was Hemingway's second-in-command on the Pilar. In Islands in the Stream *he is known as the character Henry Wood. He later became owner and reputedly became a millionaire, with Guest Aerovias de Mexico, S.A., the smallest of three Mexican airlines.*

John Edgar Hoover helped establish the FBI in 1935 and was the FBI's first Director. He modernized it and established innovations such as the ultimately massive collection of fingerprint records. Respected throughout much, but not all of his tenure, he was "Director for Life." He was ultimately accused of wiretapping, and violating the civil rights of those who were perceived to be enemies of his Bureau.

The FBI maintained files on political activists, writers such as Hemingway, John Steinbeck and many others, and did surveillance on political "enemies." Many critics believed the FBI under Hoover exceeded its jurisdiction and mandate on any number of occasions. Presidents Truman, Kennedy and Johnson tried—and failed—to get him to retire. Rumors circulated—and still circulate—that he may have been a homosexual or a crossdresser or both. He remained a bachelor throughout his life.

Hoover died May 2, 1972, still in office.

Because of the length and ultimately controversial nature of his tenure, Directors of the FBI are now limited to ten years in office.

A selection of the original files

The following are pages from the original FBI files on Hemingway.

1. First page of the Hemingway file, to J. Edgar Hoover office from R. G. Leddy, Legal Attache in the American Embassy, Havana, dated October 8, 1942.

2. Memo from J. Edgar Hoover, December 19, 1942 to two colleagues in the FBI in Washington, D.C. The first paragraph reads:

   In regard to Mr. Ladd's memorandum of the 17th instant concerning the use of Ernest Hemingway by the United States Ambassador to Cuba, I of course realize the complete undesirability of this sort of a connection or relationship. Certainly Hemingway is the last man, in my estimation, to be used in any such capacity. His judgment is not of the best, and if his sobriety is the same as it was some years ago, that is certainly questionable.

3. The first page of a memorandum dated April 27, 1943 by FBI administrator D.M. Ladd accusing Hemingway of being "connected with various so-called Communist front organizations" (first paragraph, underlined material).

4. Memorandum dated August 13, 1943 from R.G. Leddy, Legal Attache at the American Embassy, Havana, to J. Edgar Hoover. The FBI knows that Hemingway is writing a book (presumably *Islands in the Stream*). Leddy writes:

> We are not yet informed as to what role the representatives of the FBI will play, but in view of Hemingway's known sentiments, will probably be portrayed as the dull, heavy-footed unimaginative policeman type.

The legal term for the blacked-out material is *redactions*.

5. J. Edgar Hoover writes to S.I.S. #396—presumably R. D. Leddy, the Legal Attache in the American Embassy in Havana, October 14, 1943. The last paragraph reads:

> It is suggested that this letter should be destroyed when it has served your purpose.

6. Memorandum dated September 20, 1943, from L.D. Ladd indicating (bottom of first paragraph) that Hemingway continued operations in Cuba on behalf of the United States Naval Attache; that is, operations consisting of cruising the waters off the coast of Cuba in a small boat for the purposes of ascertaining the extent of enemy submarine activities.

7. Cover page one (of two pages), dated (probably August) 30, 1949, for a "blind memorandum" to be sent to the Office of the Secretary of Defense in response to a FBI file check on Hemingway.

8. and 9. Two pages of a "blind memorandum" sent to the Office of the Secretary of Defense. This is on blank paper—no FBI

letterhead was been used, although the stamp at the bottom of the page states: PROPERTY OF FBI.

10. Memorandum from the SAC (Special Agent in Charge, or FBI Bureau Chief) in Minneapolis, Jan. 13, 1961, indicating that Hemingway had been a patient at the Mayo Clinic, Rochester, Minnesota. Hemingway was convinced the FBI was following him, or was "concerned about an FBI investigation."

Ernest Hemingway committed suicide six months later, in Ketchum, Idaho.

For additional description and analysis of FBI surveillance of Hemingway in his post-Cuba years, see Thomas Fensch, *Orwell in America*, pp. 127-131.

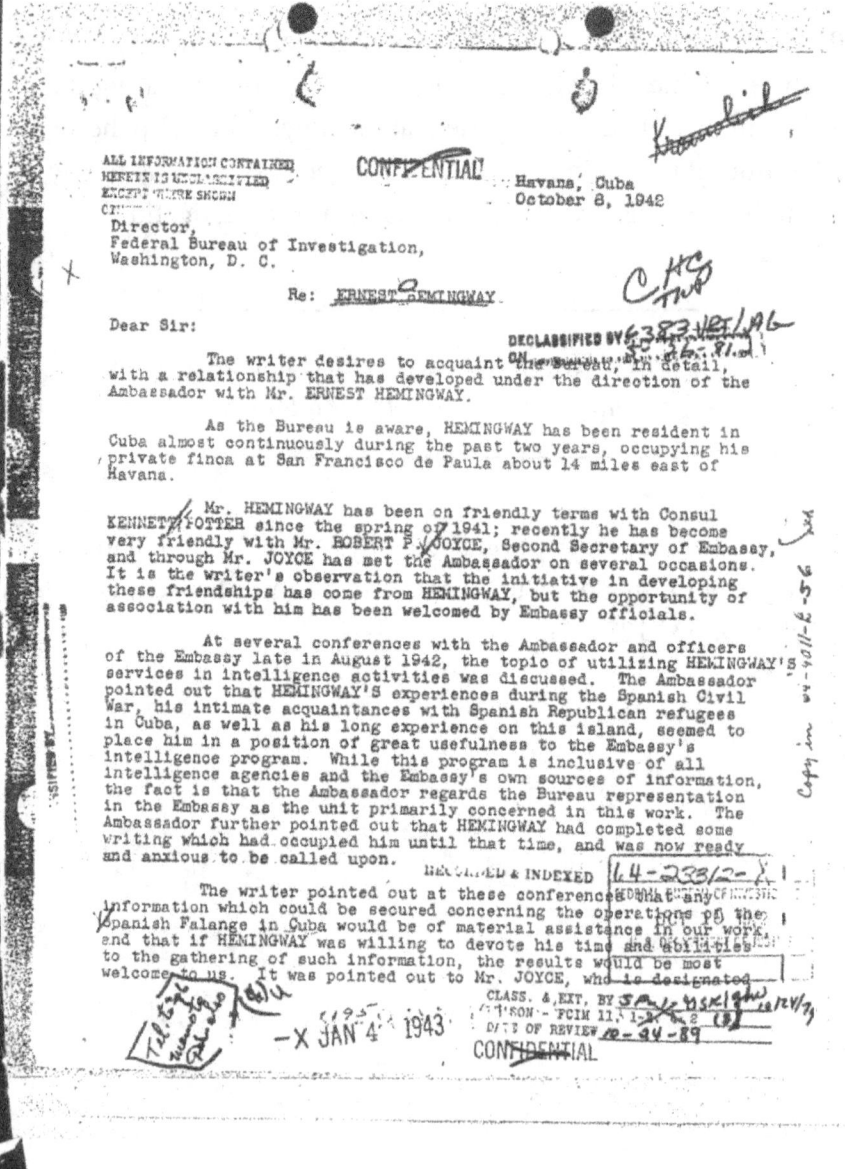

1. *First page of the Hemingway file, to J. Edgar Hoover office, October 8, 1942*

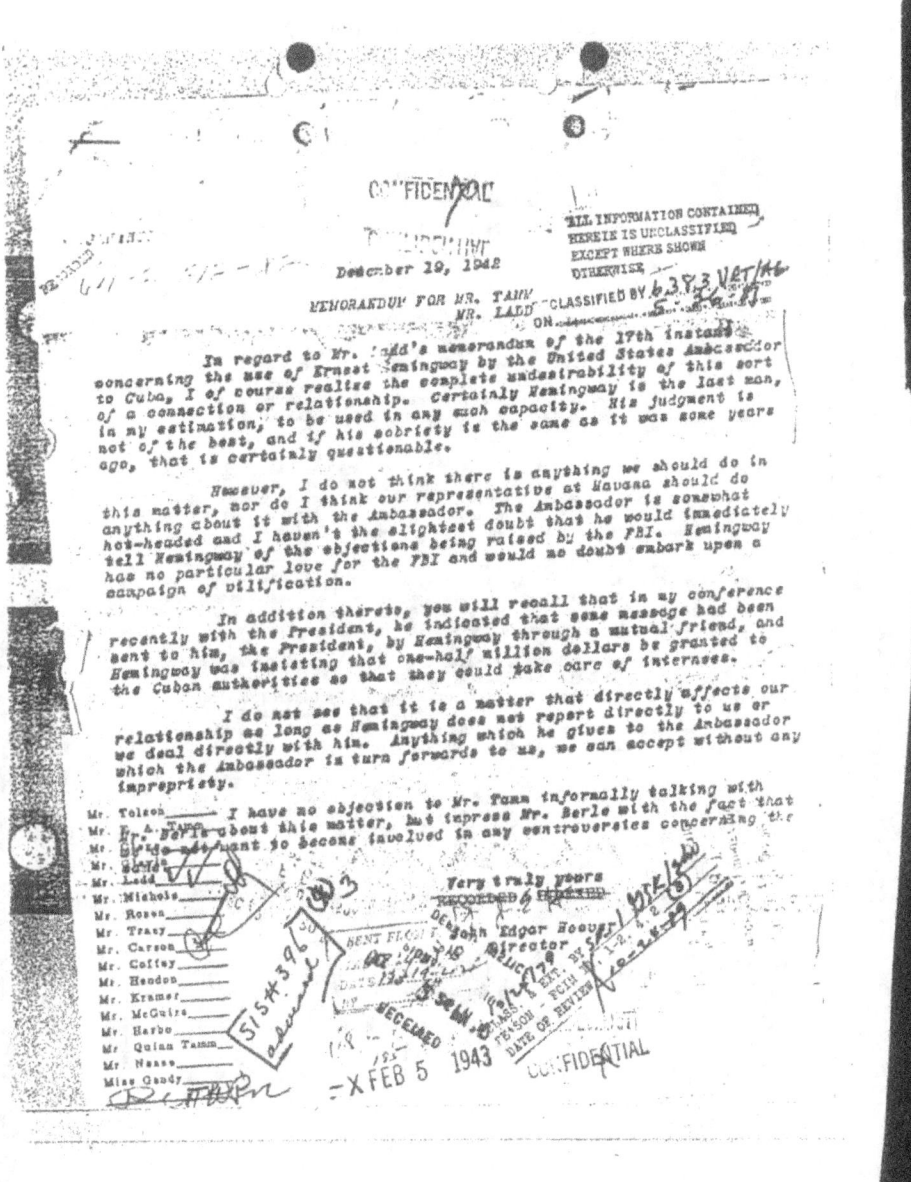

2. Memo from J. Edgar Hoover, December 19, 1942

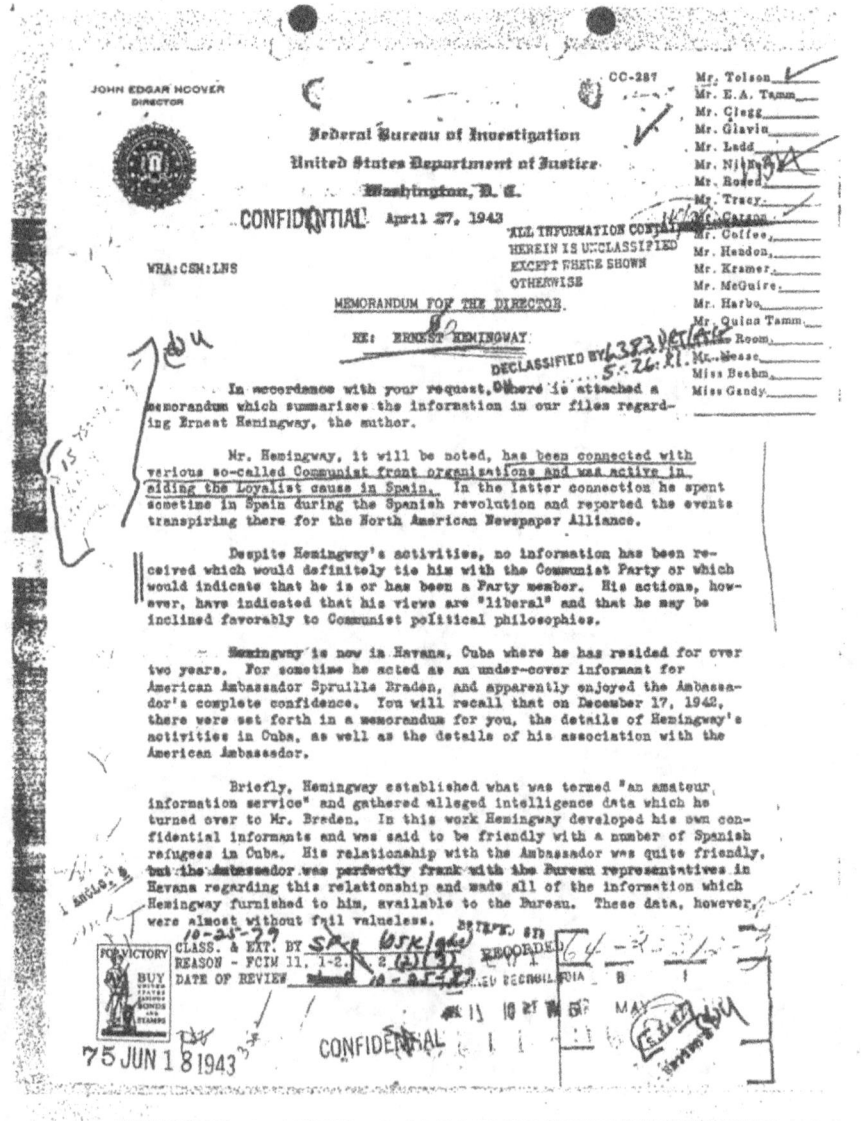

3. First page of a memorandum dated April 27, 1943 by FBI administrator D.M. Ladd

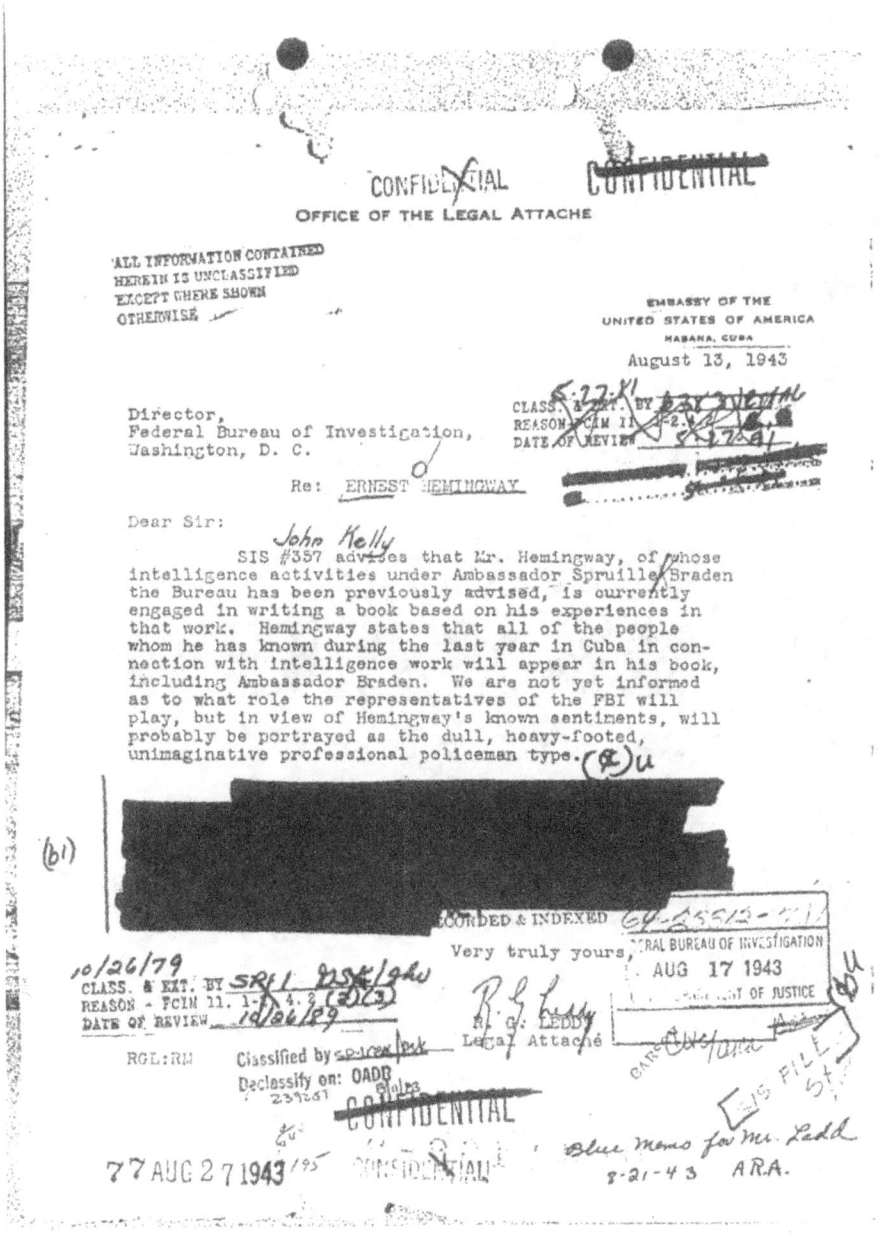

4. *Memorandum dated August 13, 1943 from R.G. Leddy, Legal Attache at the American Embassy, Havana, to J. Edgar Hoover.*

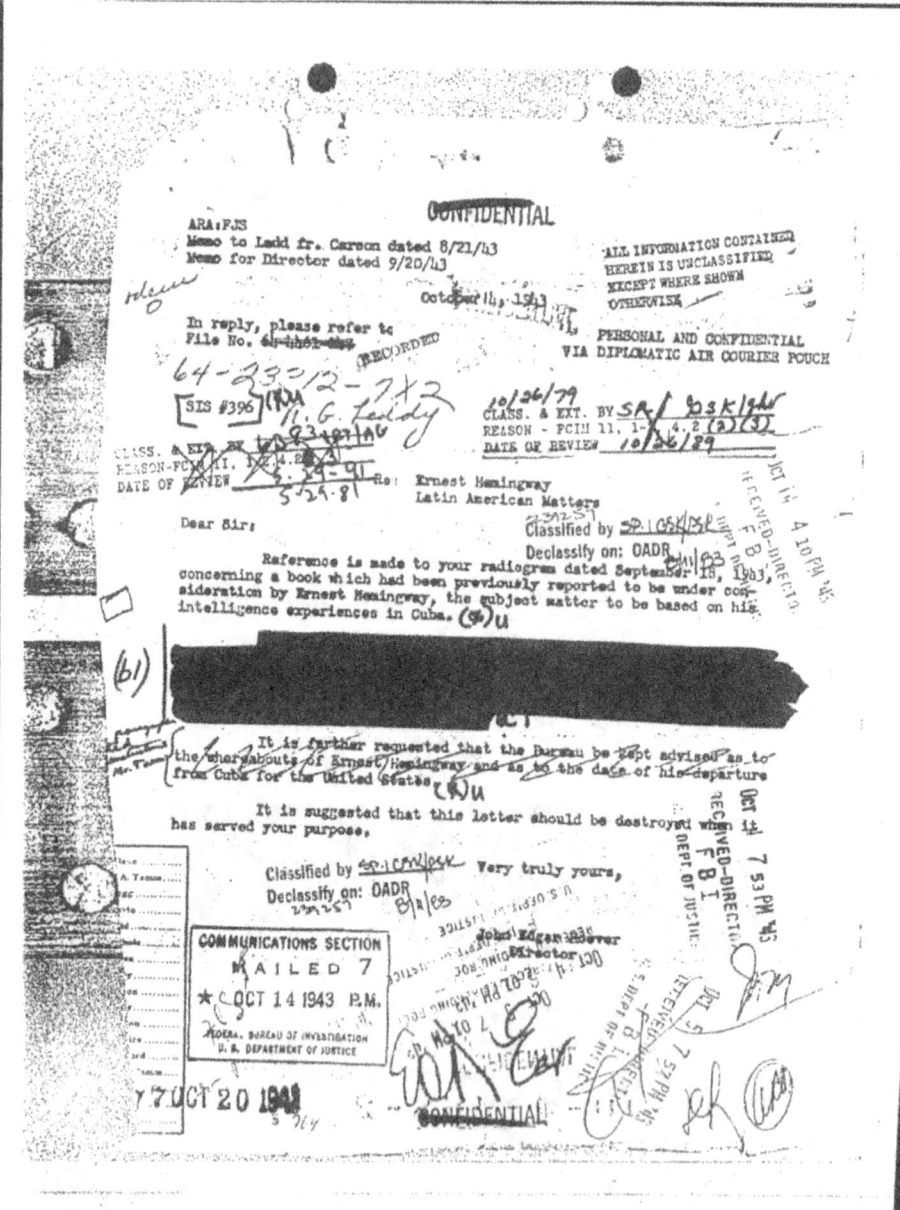

5. *J. Edgar Hoover writes to S.I.S. #396*

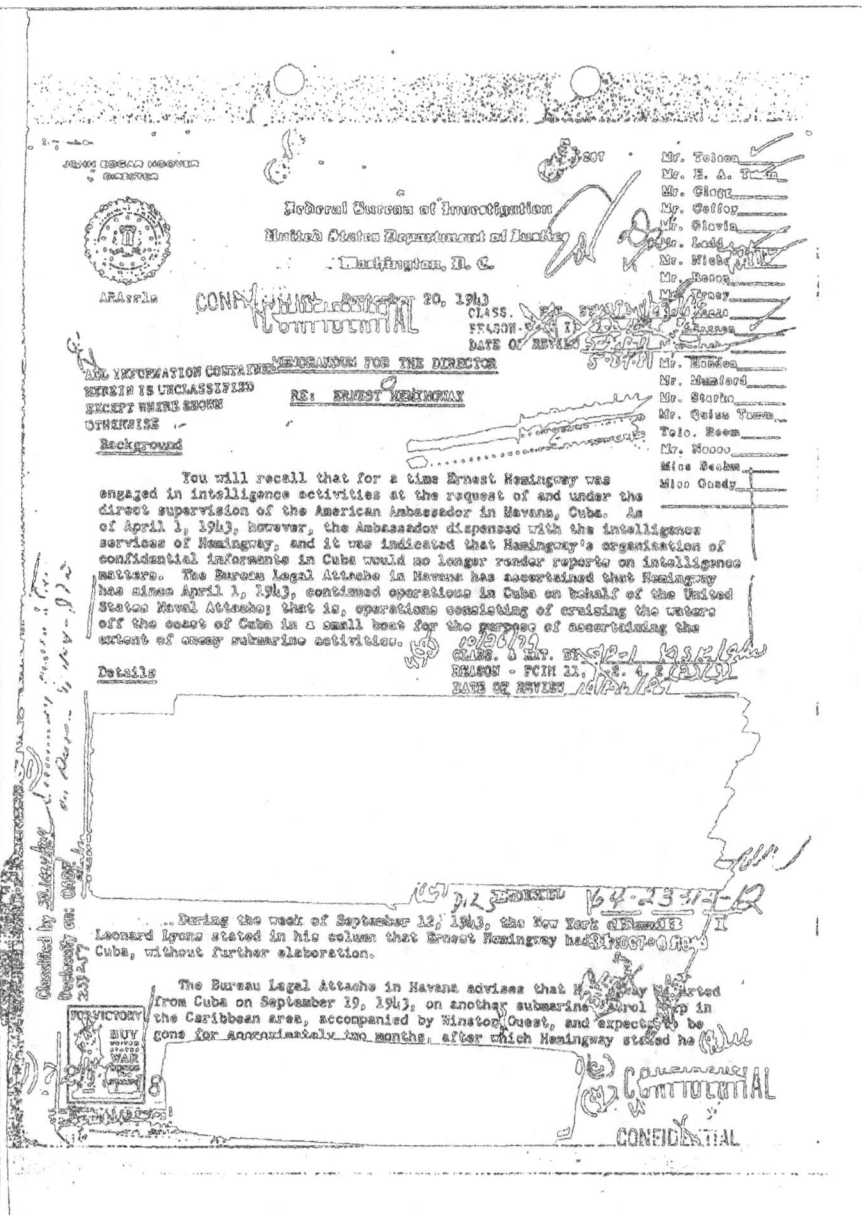

6. *Memorandum dated September 20, 1943, from L.D. Ladd*

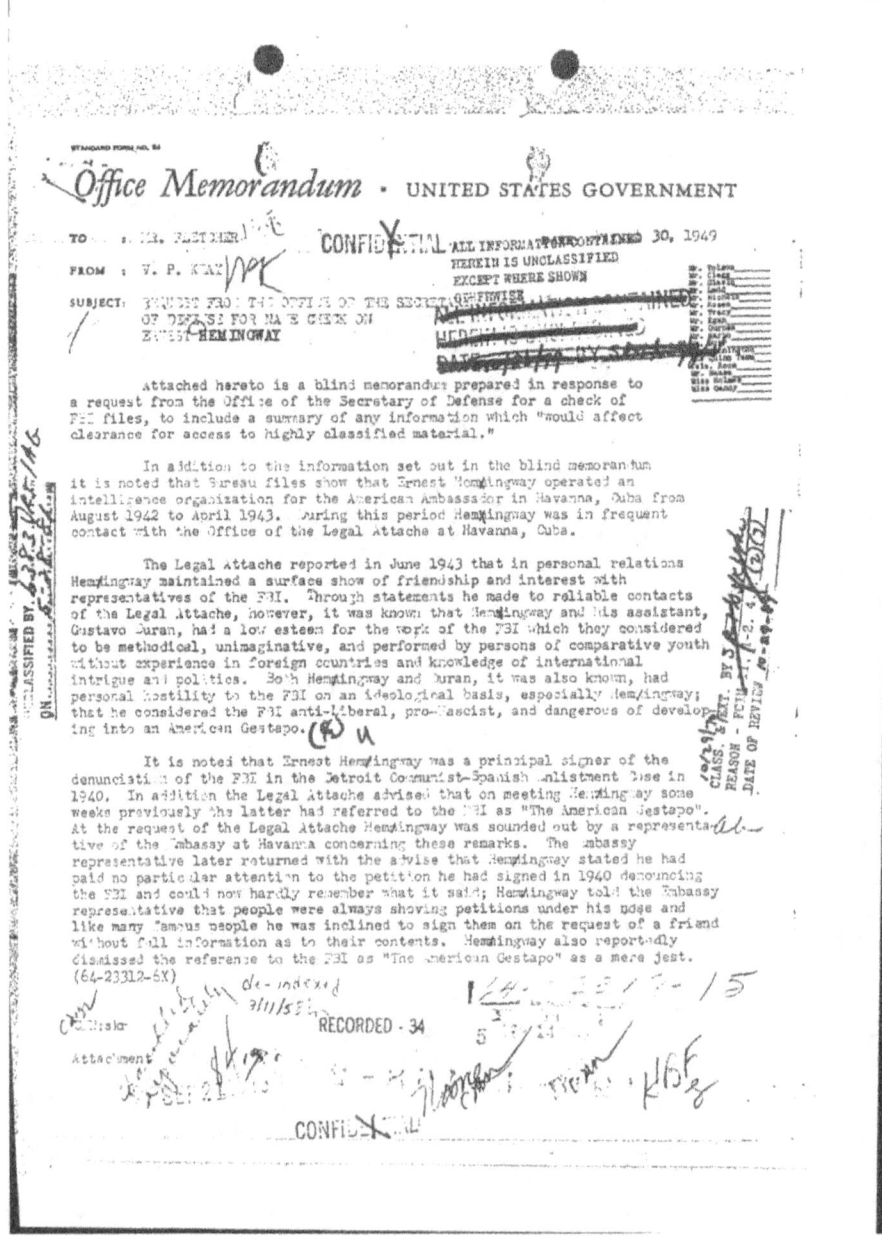

7. Cover page of a "blind memorandum" to be sent to the Office of the Secretary of Defense in response to a FBI file check on Hemingway.

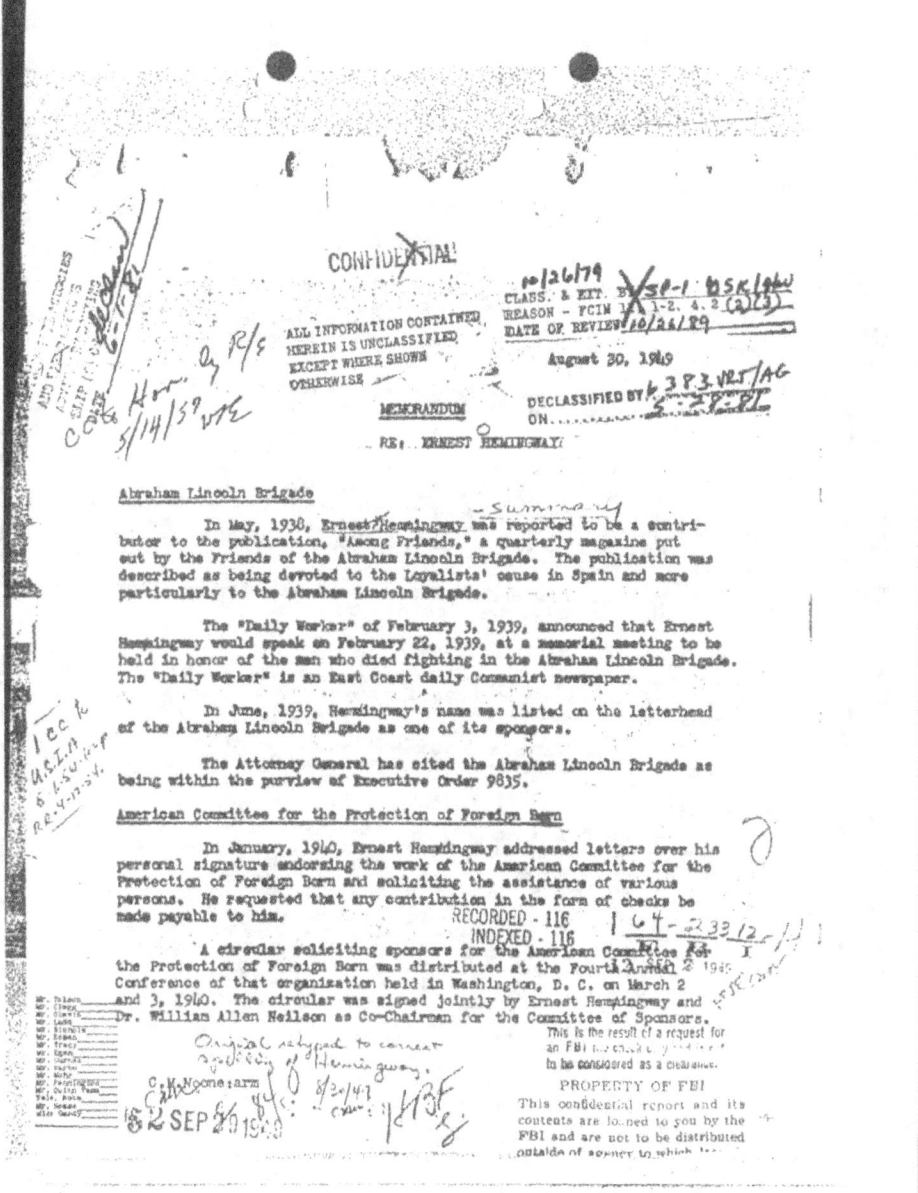

8. Page of a "blind memorandum" sent to the Office of the Secretary of Defense

CONFIDENTIAL

Ernest Hemingway was listed as a sponsor of the American Committee for the Protection of Foreign Born as of August, 1940. He was also listed as a sponsor for the Fifth National Conference of the American Committee for the Protection of Foreign Born which was scheduled to be held in Atlantic City on March 29 and 30, 1941.

The American Committee for the Protection of Foreign Born was declared by the Attorney General to be within the purview of Executive Order 9835.

American Rescue Ship Mission

The January 16, 1941, issue of the "Daily Worker" published an article bearing the headline, "Hemingway Reaffirms Backing of Rescue Ship Mission." The article quoted a cable received from Hemingway in Havana in which he expressed the sincere hope that a ship would be obtained "as soon as it's humanly possible to do so."

The American Rescue Ship Mission has been declared by the Attorney General to be within the purview of Executive Order 9835.

League of American Writers

On February 21, 1941, Ernest Hemingway was reported as being a Vice-President and a member of the Board of Directors of the League of American Writers, Incorporated.

The League of American Writers has been cited by the Attorney General as being within the purview of Executive Order 9835.

(64-23312-3)

Miscellaneous

A reliable informant has reported that during the period 1942 – 1943, Ernest Hemingway repeatedly asserted that he was anti-Communist and that he was as much opposed to the Communist influence in the Spanish war as he was to the Fascist. (64-23312-6-p.7)

A reliable informant has reported that in September, 1943, Ernest Hemingway was discussing certain newspaper articles which attacked the United States Army for refusing to admit to the Officers' Training School individuals who had fought in the Abraham Lincoln Brigade in the Spanish Civil War. According to the informant, Hemingway took exception and stated that the United States Army was perfectly justified in the action which was taken inasmuch as each individual who had been refused admission to the Officers' Training School was an out-and-out Communist.

(64-23312-10)

Blind Memorandum for Transmittal
to the Office of the Secretary
of Defense.

CONFIDENTIAL

9. Page of a "blind memorandum" sent to the Office of the Secretary of Defense

```
FD-36 (Rev. 12-13-56)

                                FBI

                                Date: 1/13/61

Transmit the following in _____PLAIN_____
                                (Type in plain text or code)
Via _____AIRTEL_____
                                (Priority or Method of Mailing)

TO:     DIRECTOR, FBI          PERSONAL ATTENTION
FROM:   SAC, MINNEAPOLIS
RE:     ERNEST HEMINGWAY
        INFORMATION CONCERNING

    ERNEST HEMINGWAY, the author, has been a patient at Mayo
Clinic, Rochester, Minnesota, and is presently at St. Mary's
Hospital in that city. He has been at the Clinic for several
weeks, and is described as a problem. He is seriously ill,
both physically and mentally, and at one time the doctors
were considering giving him electro-shock therapy treatments.
                            Mayo Clinic, advised to
eliminate publicity and contacts by newsmen, the Clinic had
suggested that Mr. HEMINGWAY register under the alias GEORGE
SEVIER.         stated that Mr. HEMINGWAY is now
worried about his registering under an assumed name, and is
concerned about an FBI investigation.        stated that
inasmuch as this worry was interfering with the treatments
of Mr. HEMINGWAY, he desired authorization to tell HEMINGWAY
that the FBI was not concerned with his registering under
an assumed name.         was advised that there was no
objection.

3 - Bureau
1 - Minneapolis
WHW:RSK
(4)
```

10. *Memorandum from the SAC (Special Agent in Charge, or FBI Bureau Chief) in Minneapolis, Jan. 13, 1961*

2
Islands in the Stream

It is perhaps the clearest *roman a clef* in American literature; *Islands in the Stream* is the very definition of *roman a clef*.

First published in 1970, the book is divided into three sections: Bimini, pages 1–200; Cuba, 203–327 and At Sea, 331–466.

Hemingway's protagonist, Thomas Hudson *is* Hemingway; in age, in height, weight and bearing, and, most particularly, emotionally. We see a remarkable picture of Hemingway as Thomas Hudson.

Hudson remembers the women in his life, the ones he left; the ones he never should have left:

> But why did I ever leave Tom's mother in the first place? You better not think about that, he told himself. That is one thing you had better not think about. And these are fine children that you got from the other one. Very strange and very complicated and you know how many of those good qualities come from her. She is a fine woman and you never should have left her either. Then he said to himself, Yes I had to. (pp. 7)

And then there are the Hudson sons.

Hudson is planning a vacation, with his three boys coming in, to spend time together:

> Thomas Hudson was familiar with the pattern by now and finally there was the usual compromise. The two younger boys would come to the island to visit their father for five weeks and then leave to sail from New York, student class, on a French Line boat to join their mother in Paris where she would have bought a few necessary clothes. They would be in charge of their older brother, young Tom, on the trip. Young Tom would then join *his* mother, who was making a picture in the south of France. (pp. 6)

Hemingway had one son, John, with his first wife Hadley Richardson Hemingway and two sons, Patrick and Gregory, with his second wife Pauline Pfeiffer Hemingway.

Hemingway may have Paul Gauguin (1848–1903) in mind for Hudson. Gauguin left Europe for Tahiti to paint local subjects; Thomas Hudson left civilization for Bimini to paint local scenes.

Early in the book, there is this dialogue between Hudson and Bobby, a local bartender:

> "You sell those pictures you paint all the time?"
> "They sell pretty good now."
> "People paying money for pictures of Uncle Edward.
> "Pictures of Negroes in the water. Negroes on land. Negroes in boats. Turtle boats. Sponge boats. Squalls making up. Water spouts. Schooners that got wrecked. Schooners building. Everything they could see free. They really buy them?" (pp. 16–17)

And the cats. There is a whole section in *Islands in the Stream* about Thomas Hudson's cats. Boise and Big Goats and

Princessa and Willy and Friendless and Friendless's Brother (who was actually Friendless's sister). And Littless, Furhouse and Taskforce, and Uncle Woolfie. And how one of Hudson's sons had wanted Boise, who was given to the boy when it was a kitten, while Hudson was drinking at a Havana bar, the boy in tow, and how much later, Hudson remembered, the cat had outlived the boy, who was killed with his brother and their mother in an auto accident in Europe.

And, of course, they were all Hemingway's cats (pp. 203–222).

(In the Introduction to *Hemingway in Cuba*, Gabriel Garcia Marquez writes, "In Finca Vigia Hemingway had nine thousand books, besides four dogs and 54 cats." [pp. 11], but Noberto Fuentes says the number was "57 cats at Finca Vigia, 43 large ones and 14 small ones." [pp. 79])

Islands in the Stream elicited considerable attention when it was released in October, 1970.

Scribners sent out advance reading copies to all major reviewers, with publicity material, and it appeared as the main selection of the Book of the Month Club.

It sold 100,000 copies in the first three months after publication and appeared on the best seller lists for a half year (Meyers, pp. 484).

Reviewers had much to consider: it was common knowledge the book was unfinished at the time of Hemingway's death; what was unknown was the extent that Mary Hemingway and the editors at Scribners may have edited the manuscript into publishable shape and how it might fit into the Hemingway canon.

In *The Immediate Critical Reception of Ernest Hemingway*, Frank L. Ryan wrote (and quoted the review by John Aldridge in *The Saturday Review of Literature* of Oct. 10, 1970):

The posthumous publication of a novel by a world famous novelist is of course an event of considerable interest and John Aldridge summed up the heavy atmospheric pressure surrounding the publication of *Islands in the Stream* (1970);

Knowing that this may well be the last new Hemingway novel we may ever see, one approaches it with a mixture of wariness, awe, and considerable anxiety, hoping that through some charity of the gods it will turn out to be very good, but knowing also the chances against the novel's being other than very bad.

Judging from the reviews, the gods were not charitable and Aldridge's somber conjecture about the novel "being bad" proved to be an accurate reflection of the reviewers' rejections. However, though it was a rejection, and a frigid one, there hung of it an atmosphere of courtesy, restraint, and even sadness which was new in Hemingway criticism. Reviewers expanded their interest beyond the book itself to include the status of Hemingway's literary reputation, the creative and editing problems involved in the publication of the novel, most significant, problems concerning Hemingway as writer, myth, person, (pp. 35–36)

Reviews appeared in: *America; The Atlantic Monthly; Best Sellers; Book World; The Boston Globe; Catholic World; The Chicago Sun Times; Choice; The Christian Science Monitor; Commentary; Commonweal; Contemporary Literature; The Economist; Harper's; Library Journal; The Miami Herald; Life; The Nation; The National Observer; National Review; The New Republic; The New Statesman; The New York Review of Books; The New York Times Book Review; Newsweek; Paris Match;*

Publishers Weekly; The Salt Lake Tribune; The San Francisco Chronicle; Saturday Review of Literature; The Seattle Times; The Spectator; Time; The Virginia Quarterly Review, Yacht and surely many others.

Here, in alphabetic order, are excerpts from selected major reviews:

A Double Life, Half Told

Thomas Hudson is not a hero of myth. He is based on Hemingway himself, as most of the other heroes are (except Santiago and Harry Morgan), but in fact he represents only one side of the author: I mean the mask or persona that Hemingway adopted in his relations with the world. Thus, he is brave, competent, wise in a fatherly fashion, and able to hold his liquor — as Hemingway truly was in life — but those qualities in the author were mingled with others that make him an endless study. Hudson gives hardly a hint of having deeper qualities except for a feeling of despair, regarding which the author brings forward a drastic explanation: it was caused, he gives us to understand, by the death of Hudson's three sons. But the reader is likely to feel that the despair of longer standing, based as it seems to be on the same feeling in the author, and that the sons have served as a blood sacrifice to the exigencies of fiction.

That is the weaker side of *Islands in the Stream*, but one must add that it is a bold, often funny, always swashbuckling book that only Hemingway could have written. It gives one a new respect for the efforts of his later years. Handicapped as he was by injuries and admirers, he continued almost to the end a double life, playing the great man in public — and playing the part superbly — then standing alone at his work table, humble and persistent, while he tried to summon back his early powers. At the very end, he found that he had been too deeply wounded to write even a single sentence after standing there all day. Nevertheless, that private, disciplined, puzzled, and finally despairing self of his now seems more appealing than his brilliant persona. It has a different sort of greatness, in some ways resembling that of his own Santiago.

— Malcolm Cowley, *The Atlantic Monthly,* Dec., 1970.

Those who wish to can find flaws, can complain that the three divisions are not perfectly wed, that some of the scenes verge on self-parody …. But they would be wrong.

This is a big, impressive, and haunting book; it may not be the masterpiece we wanted, but the particular world of Hemingway is much with us in these pages. The novel is certain to be in demand in all libraries, and it deserves many readers.

— C.W. Mann, *Library Journal,* September 1, 1970.

Papa's disappointing 'big one'

Reminiscent of the more ambitious suspense novels *Islands in the Stream* is the sort of action-cum-philosophy story that most people enjoy, but like the man who discovers that he has been speaking prose all his life, the reader soon discovers he is in the presence of Literature. The rhetoric is louder than the gunfire; the action is only the Purple Heart of art. You could no more mistake the book for mere entertainment than you could mistake Gertrude Stein for Sophie Tucker.

* * *

In an incredible interlude of carelessness—or perhaps because of the death wish Hemingway seems to have projected onto him—Hudson is fatally wounded. For whatever reason, his death falls so far short of tragic inevitability as to seem dramatically meaningless. As he dies, cursing the fatal bullets for cutting short his career, one of his crew pronounces his epitaph: "You never understand anybody that loves you."

The line sums up not only Hudson, but Hemingway himself, for he certainly did not understand either love or people. What he did understand was that life is rich in proportion to what we put in it. This affirmation, this anguished, old-fashioned faith, reaches and moves us in spite of the book's many shortcomings. In fact, it may be precisely this—Hemingway's insatiable hunger for experience—that flawed his rendering of it.

— Anatole Broyard, *Life*, Oct. 9, 1970.

The Novel in the Drawer

Ernest Hemingway once declared that a writer's best gift was a "built-in shock-proof shit detector." He himself had a good one and he was not above using those of others, like Ezra Pound, Gertrude Stein and F. Scott Fitzgerald. So just a certain amount of bad Hemingway was published during his lifetime—mainly during his *Esquire* period, and then later in *The Fifth Column* and *Across the River and Into the Trees*. Now more of it than has been ever before been brought together in one book which has been published as something of a novel, *Islands in the Stream*.

According to Philip Young and Charles Mann's inventory of the Hemingway manuscripts, there had been until now some 3,000 pages of unpublished writings. The present "novel" is made up of sections that Hemingway had labeled variously as "Sea Novel" and "The Island the Stream" — all of which amounted to three segments of seventeen, four and twenty-one chapters in manuscript. Mary Hemingway and Charles Scribner, Jr. took upon themselves the unenviable task of bringing these materials together and editing them into book shape. No one will doubt the difficulty of such a task and we will have no way of truly evaluating the job until the manuscripts are available for study; but no one who reads the book will doubt, either, that those responsible should have sent out for one of Hemingway's detectors.

For though it is a pleasure to hear Hemingway's voice once more, *Islands in the Stream* is too often mawkish, sentimental and tasteless — particularly in a long dialogue between the protagonist Thomas Hudson and a Cuban prostitute called "Honest Lil," but also in love scenes between Hudson and his cat Boise, and Hudson and his first wife. Those who have always objected to the exaggerated concerns for masculinity in Hemingway's fiction, as well as those who have viewed him as a dumb ox of a writer with but one or two crude thoughts to express, are going to use those passages as a concluding "I told you so." Those who saw him develop a style that was in itself an ethic and a way of life will wince to see the style wasted.

* * *

Even in its present form, *Islands in the Stream* is the work of an estimable writer. Its gaga humor belong with *The Torrents of Spring*, its moribund and democratic message echoes *For Whom the Bell Tolls.* Issuing from the vaults of some Manhattan bank, Hemingway's voice is still effective, hauntingly so. It takes us back to that time in our international history when men could still play at war, although they had begun to suspect it was truly a sickness unto death.

— Bernard Oldsey, *The Nation,* October 19, 1970.

How Papa Grew

Overall, it seems unlikely that Hemingway would have wanted to publish the book in this form, not merely because it needed much cutting and refining but because it so obviously anticipates *A Moveable Feast* and *The Old Man and the Sea* that it seems almost a working draft.

The real interest *Islands in the Stream* holds is as the definitive delineation of the *papier mache* Hemingway, drawn for us not by Baker or Hotchner or *Life,* but by the image himself. The central character, Thomas Hudson, a painter, is clearly to be read as Hemingway; so, to a lesser extent, is his best friend Roger Davis, a writer. Their conversations (Hemingway talking to Hemingway!) and actions are designed to reveal Hemingway in all his aspects, to create the Official Portrait.

* * *

Islands in the Stream does not offer much of anything except the legend. It provides no new keys to Hemingway's literary importance. Its narrative is competent (at narrative Hemingway was *never* incompetent), and it contains just enough flickering reminders of his wasted genius to make reading it a frustrating and saddening experience.

— Jonathan Yardley, *The New Republic,* October 10, 1970.

This book consists of material that the author during his lifetime did not see fit to publish; therefore it should not be held against him .... It is, I think, to the discredit of his publishers that no introduction (the American edition does carry a very terse, uninformative note by Mary Hemingway) offers to describe from what stage of Hemingway's tormented later career (the work) was salvaged, or to estimate what its completed design might have been, or to confess what editorial choices were exercised in the preparation of this manuscript. Rather, a gallant wreck of a novel is now paraded as the real thing.

— John Updike, *The New Statesman,* October 16, 1970.

Out of the Desk

It has been known for many years that Ernest Hemingway wrote a novel after World War II of which "The Old Man and the Sea" was a section, the only portion to be published. "Islands in the Stream" is the rest of it. It is a very bad novel with a few bright moments. Its central character, Thomas Hudson, is a persona for Hemingway. During three distinct episodes the painter is at the center of the novel's action, judging himself and his talent and his broken marriage and his three sons and his courage in the war against the Germans. But his judgments are usually tentative and often silly. Hemingway's prose is uncharacteristically loose-gaited, as though the author let his attention to it wander.

But a review of this book calls for special ground rules. It was not published during Hemingway's lifetime because in its unrevised state he didn't think it was good enough to be published. No one can say with any certainty, or least no one has said, what he might have done with the book had he not shot himself in 1961. Perhaps he decided it was a miserable botch. Most serious writers have written miserable botches; no one would deny them that necessary privilege. It is certain that Hemingway would have tightened his sentences, even if he had let it go forth. Since he was not give that opportunity, we must read his work with the indulgent eye required of a man who has just burgled a friend's desk to read the friend's mail.

* * *

Shadow: The first section, in which Thomas Hudson fishes with his sons before the war, is much the best. There is a description of a fight against a swordfish that is superb; there are a few passages of inspired comic dialogue. But Thomas Hudson himself is a shadow, a talking machine, an instrument of rote memory, a palimpsest upon which Hemingway writes and Hemingway erases. Two of the sons die off stage in an auto accident to provide a suitable occasion for the hero's despondency. The third is killed during the war for a similar reason.

— Geoffrey Wolff, *Newsweek,* October 12, 1970.

100-proof Old Ernest, most of it anyway

[This] is a complete, well-rounded novel, a contender with [the author's] very best. It has his characteristic blend of strong-running narrative and reflective memento mori and it is 100-proof Old Ernest, most of it.... In the first two parts there is a kind of leisureliness, a plentitude of incident and conversation. Hudson, like many Hemingway heroes, is an alter ego... [But he] is splendidly realized both as a man and as a painter. Hemingway's brilliant descriptive talent frames one small superb picture after another in Hudson's eyes, to make him that rare thing in literature, a believable artist.

As a man, he is efficient and capable, but he always falls just a little short of the heroic effort that events demand of him. The verge of failure is always close — and this gives the story much of its quiet tension ... The third (and finest) section, 'At Sea,' goes from the desperation of inaction to a long, tense, desperate stalk [Published] nine years after [Hemingway's] death, [this is] a book much finer than any the young contenders can write.

— Robie Macauley, *The New York Times Book Review*, Oct. 4, 1970.

Papa Watching

Those who forged through last year's biography by Carlos Baker may recall that Ernest Hemingway, in the late 1940s and early 1950s, was engaged in writing three loosely linked narratives. Somewhat Delphically, he referred to them as The Sea When Young, The Sea When Absent and The Sea in Being. The first two apparently dealt with a famous painter named Thomas Hudson enjoying a Bimini vacation with his teen-aged sons and then, later, hunting German submarines around the Caribbean in his fishing boat during World War II. In his sins, sons, sub chasing, and syntax, Thomas Hudson greatly resembled another straight and true artist named Ernest Hemingway.

Hollywood props. Hemingway later published The Sea in Being separately — as The Old Man and the Sea —

and, largely as a result, won a Nobel Prize. But he never released the Thomas Hudson narratives. Now they have been made public by Scribners and Mary Hemingway, admittedly only after long deliberation. The decision may be challenged, for Islands in the Stream is in many ways a stunningly bad book. At his best, Ernest Hemingway the writer knew that Papa Hemingway the public figure was his own worst literary creation. One suspects he would have eventually got round to slashing Islands in the Stream back by a third or a half its present length. Yet for Papa watchers and Hemingway readers the book is welcome enough. Like the recent sale of backlot stage props from old Hollywood films, its publication seems a commendable act of commerce and nostalgic piety.

— Timothy Foote, *Time,* Oct. 5, 1970.

Complete versions of the reviews excerpted here, and others, can be accessed at any major library; some of these reviews can now be found by publication, date and author, on the internet.

Denouement...

In *Islands in the Stream,* written earlier but published in 1970, Hemingway writes about Thomas Hudson drinking in the Floridita bar in downtown Havana, and who he saw there:

> It stared at noon at the Floridita and he had drunk first with Cuban politicians that had dropped in, nervous for a quick one; with sugar planters and rice planters; with Cuban government functionaries, drinking through their lunch hour; with second and third secretaries of Embassy, shepherding someone to the Floridita; with the inescapable FBI men, pleasant and all trying to look so average, clean-cut-young-American that they stood out as clearly as though they had worn a bureau shoulder patch on their white linen or seersucker suits. (pp. 215)

In *Hemingway in Cuba,* published in 1982 and translated into English and republished in the U.S. in 1984, Norberto Fuentes quotes Hemingway about who he sees in Havana:

> "There are people there from all the states and from places you have lived," he wrote, "There are also Navy ships in, cruise ships, Customs and Immigration agents, gamblers, embassy characters, aspiring writers, firmly

or poorly established writers, senators on the town, the physicians and surgeons who come from conventions. Lions, Elks, Moose, Shriners, American Legion members, Knights of Columbus, beauty contest winners, characters who have gotten into a little trouble and pass a note in by the doorman, characters who get killed next week, characters who will be killed next year, the F.B.I., former F.B.I. occasionally your bank manager and two others guys, not to mention your Cuban friends." (pp. 9–10)

In *Papa Hemingway*, published in 1966, A.E. Hotchner has this episode about Hemingway, apparently before he entered the Mayo Clinic. Hotchner and Hemingway and a friend, Duke MacMullen, are driving toward Ketchum, Idaho:

"Vernon Lord wanted to come but I wouldn't let him."
"Why?"
"The Feds."
"What?"
"Feds. They tailed us all the way. Ask Duke."
"Well…there was a car in the back of us out of Hailey…"
"That's why I wanted to get you out of the bar. Was afraid they'd make their move and pick us up there."
"But Ernest, that car turned off at Picabo," Duke said. "Probably took the back road. That would take them longer, so I wanted to be out of Shoshone when they got there."
"But Papa," I said, trying to collect myself, "why are federal agents pursuing you?"
"It's the worst hell. The goddamnedest hell. They've bugged everything. That's why were using Duke's car. Mine's bugged. Everything's bugged. Can't use the phone.

Mail intercepted. What put me on to it was that phone call to you. You remember we got disconnected. That tipped their hand." (pp. 266)

Readers could be forgiven for not noticing these similar episodes, even if the three books were read back-to-back-to-back. Those reading *Papa Hemingway*, when it was published in 1966, would assume Hemingway was paranoid—paranoid and delusional and perhaps dysfunctional. He was treated at the Mayo Clinic for uncontrolled high blood pressure, liver trouble, diabetes and depression. And given electro-shock treatments, which destroyed his memory and his ability to write. Nearly fifty years later, some other treatment regimen might be more effective, but electro-shock treatments were prescribed then—and administered.

In December, 1960, he was given eleven to fifteen electric shock treatments. Subsequently, in April, 1961, he returned to the Mayo Clinic and was given ten additional shock treatments. (Meyers, 547–551). They were horrific; very close to Frankenstein scenes in mid-twentieth century American medicine.

They cost Hemingway the rest of his career, his soul and, six months later, his life.

And after the treatments at the Mayo Clinic, what shards of memory did he have left? Perhaps only the strongest memories of his past survived. Of Hadley, of living in Paris, of Pauline, of Martha, then Mary. Living in Finca Vigia, drinking in downtown Havana, writing, chasing Nazi submarines on the Pilar, and his later years.

And the FBI.

Hemingway surely knew he was under constant surveillance by the FBI during the years he lived in Cuba, before he left to cover the war in Europe and liberate the Ritz bar in Paris.

Then shadowed again, after the Hemingways moved to Ketchum, Idaho. And when he became seriously physically and mentally ill.

The FBI had shadowed him *before* he entered the Mayo Clinic. Jeffery Meyers writes:

> The FBI had, in fact, tracked Hemingway to the walls of the Mayo Clinic and discussed his case with his psychiatrist. The agents *were* following him and he knew it, and was much more realistic and perceptive than his wife and friend. Dr. Rome's contact with the FBI gave substance to Hemingway's fear "that one of the interns was a Fed in disguise." The FBI file on Hemingway proves that even paranoids have real enemies. (pp. 543)

The doctor who spoke with the FBI was Howard Rome, who was treating Hemingway. There seems to be a major question of medical ethics involved when a psychiatrist divulges confidential information about a patient to an organization such as the FBI. And, following his suicide, there was probably cause of a major lawsuit for medical malpractice, but Mary Hemingway chose not to pursue it.

Did the FBI follow him to Ketchum, Idaho, as he suspected and indicated to Hotchner and MacMullen? It seems plausible.

Did his memory of — or his paranoia about — the FBI trigger his suicide?

And his suicide on the morning of July 2, 1961: the last act of a man who saw it as the only way out. Was it as spontaneous as it appeared? Perhaps, but perhaps not.

He had rehearsed it years before.

At least once in front of friends and god only knows how many times in private. (Even though he apparently despised his father for committing suicide with a pistol, decades earlier.)

This remarkable episode appears in *Hemingway in Cuba* (Fuentes gives no date for this):

> The possible alternative of suicide has become an obsession with Hemingway. On more one occasion at Finca Vigia he said he would some day kill himself. He even rehearsed the way he would do it.
>
> "Look, this is how I am going to do it," he would explain to friends, according to Sotolongo.
>
> "He would then sit in his chair, barefoot, and place the butt of his Mannlicher .256 on the fiber rug of the living room between his legs. Then, leaning forward, he would rest the mouth of the gun barrel against the roof of his mouth. He would press the trigger with his big toe and we would hear the click of the gun. He would then raise his head and smile.
>
> "'This is the technique of harakiri with a gun,' he'd say. 'The palate is the softest part of the head.'" (pp. 68)

In fact, Hemingway appeared to have had suicidal thoughts throughout his entire life:

> Suicide was a recurrent theme in Hemingway's life and work. Even before his father's suicide in 1928, which profoundly influenced his ideas and emotions, he was obsessed by the theme of self-destruction. (Meyers, 555)

Is *Islands in the Stream* a bottom-shelf project? A back-of-the-file-cabinet manuscript? When it was published in 1970, every critic indicated it had flaws; many suggested major flaws. It was disconnected; the dialogue maudlin or worse. Some suggested it should have never been published; others asked how Mary Hemingway and the editors at Scribners jockeyed the text into publishable form.

Islands in the Stream is surely not at the bottom of the Hemingway canon; it can be placed above *The Torrents of Spring*, written solely to a break a contract with Boni & Liveright and it can be placed above *Across the River and Into the Trees* (which one critic famously called *Across the Street and Into the Bar*).

It is perhaps, maybe, almost, mid-range Hemingway, even as it was published. Can it be read and enjoyed today? Surely yes; to be read for the Hemingway style, for another look into his world, for the narrative, for the fishing and the Pilar and, in this case, to decipher the *roman a clef elements* of the novel.

John Steinbeck published *Cannery Row* in 1945, with this remarkable first paragraph:

> Cannery Row ... is a poem, a stink, a grating noise, a quality of light, a tone, a habit, a nostalgia, a dream. Cannery Row is the gathered and scattered, tin and iron and rust and splintered wood, chipped pavement and weedy lots and junkheaps, sardine canneries of corrugated iron, honky tonks, restaurants and whorehouses, and little crowded groceries, and laboratories and flophouses. Its inhabitants are, as the man once said, "whores, pimps, gamblers and sons of bitches," by which he meant Everybody. Had the man looked through another peephole he might have said "saints and angels and martyrs and holy men," and he would have meant the same thing, (pp. 1)

Substitute *Havana* for *Cannery Row* and the paragraph is just as accurate.

And just as evocative.

Suggestions for Further Reading

Braden, Spruille. *Diplomats and Demagogues: The Memoirs of Spruille Braden.* Arlington House, 1971.

Busch, Frederick. "Reading Hemingway Without Guilt." *The New York Times.* Jan. 12, 1992.

DePalma, Anthony *The Man Who Invented Fidel: Castro, Cuba and Herbert L. Matthews of The New York Times.* Public Affairs Press, 2006.

Dugdale, John. "Hemingway revealed as failed KGB spy" *The Guardian.* www.guardian.co.uk Thursday July 9, 2009.

FBI Files on Ernest Hemingway, www.paperlessarchives.com
Note: the paperlessarchives.com file contains the same materials as in this book, but has no additional narrative about Hemingway, nor any real analysis of the FBI files.

Fensch, Thomas, ed. *The FBI Files on John Steinbeck.* New Century Books, 2002.

_____ . *Orwell in America.* New Century Books, 2018.

Fuentes, Norberto. *Hemingway in Cuba.* Lyle Stuart, 1984.

Haynes, John Earl, Harvey Klehr and Alexander Vassiliev. *Spies: The Rise and Fall of the KGB in America.* Yale University Press, 2009.

Hemingway, Ernest. *Islands in the Stream.* Scribners, 1970.

Hemingway, Mary. *How It Was.* Knopf, 1976.

Hotcher, A.E. "Don't Touch A Moveable Feast." *The New York Times,* July 19, 2009.

_____ . *Papa Hemingway.* Random House, 1966.

Meyers, Jeffrey. *Hemingway: A Biography.* Harper & Row, 1985.

Mitgang, Herbert. *Dangerous Dossiers: Exposing the Secret War Against America's Greatest Writers.* Plume, 1996.

Mort, Terry A. *The Hemingway Patrols: Ernest Hemingway and His Hunt for U-Boats.* Scribner, 2009.

Pilkington, Ed. "Digital archives of papers rescued from Hemingway's home in Cuba is released" *The Guardian,* www.guardian.co.uk, Tuesday Jan. 6, 2009.

Reynolds, Michael. *Hemingway: The Final Years.* Norton, 1999.

Ryan, Frank L. *The Immediate Critical Reception of Ernest Hemingway.* University Press of America, 1980.

Simmons, Dan. *The Crook Factory.* Wm Morrow, 1999.

About the Author

Thomas Fensch has published four books about John Steinbeck.

His first book about Steinbeck, *Steinbeck and Covici: The Story of a Friendship,* was reviewed twice in *The New York Times,* in a daily issue and in the Sunday Book Review, by different authors, both laudatory reviews and was highly reviewed elsewhere. It is now considered one of the seminal books in Steinbeck scholarship. It won the Book of the Year award in biography from the Ohioana Library Association in late 1980.

He has also published *Conversations with John Steinbeck,* a collection of all the interviews Steinbeck gave during his lifetime; *The FBI Files on John Steinbeck* and *Essential Elements of Steinbeck.*

Fensch has also published the previously secret correspondence of John Kennedy and Nikita Khrushchev, titled *The Kennedy-Khrushchev Letters.*

He is also the author of two books about Theodor "Dr. Seuss" Geisel and two about James Thurber, and other books of nonfiction.

He has a doctorate from Syracuse University and lives outside Richmond, Virginia.

www.ingramcontent.com/pod-product-compliance
Lightning Source LLC
Chambersburg PA
CBHW070602010526
44118CB00012B/1428